2024 UK Ninja Air Fryer Cookbook

2000 Days Quick, Flavorful, Energy-Efficient Ninja Air Fryer Recipes for Beginners | With European Measurements & UK Ingredients

Rhonda J. Askew

Contents

Chapter 3 Family Favourites (British Classics) …………………………… 19

Chapter 9 Desserts 67

Chapter 1: Air Fryer Basic Guide

What are Air fryers?

Have you ever wondered about air fryers? No, they don't fry air! They're like small kitchen gadgets that use hot air to cook your food. Think of them as little ovens with a super-powerful fan. This fan makes your food cook quickly and get all crispy.

Using an air fryer is easy-peasy. Just put your food in a basket, choose how hot you want it, and for how long. Ta-da! Your food starts cooking. The air fryer spreads the hot air around your food, so it cooks evenly.

The cool thing is, air fryers don't need much oil. That's good because it makes your food healthier than deep frying. They can cook all kinds of stuff: like French fries, chicken nuggets, fish, veggies, frozen things, and even desserts.

Still not sure how they work? No problem, here's another simple way to understand it:

- The air fryer uses a hot element to make the air inside warm.

- A fan blows the hot air around your food, so it gets cooked on all sides.

- The hot air also takes away the wetness from your food, so it gets nice and crispy.

- The basket has little holes to let extra oil and grease drop out. That makes air frying better for you!

Advantages of Air fryers.

In this book we will be discussing about some less-talked-about advantages of Air fryers , they can be quite appealing for various reasons:

• Even Heating: Air fryers excel in distributing heat evenly. This means your food cooks consistently, reducing the risk of unevenly cooked or burnt portions.

• Space-Saving: Air fryers are compact and don't take up much counter space. They're an excellent choice for kitchens with limited room for large appliances.

• Preserving Nutrients: The rapid cooking process in air fryers can help retain more of the nutrients in your food compared to traditional methods that might lead to nutrient loss due to prolonged cooking times.

• Reduced Odors: Air fryers tend to produce fewer cooking odors than stovetop frying or baking in conventional ovens, helping your kitchen stay fresh.

• Customizable Cooking: Many air fryers offer various settings and customizable options, allowing you to fine-tune your cooking to achieve the exact results you desire.

• Healthier Cooking for Seniors: Air fryers can be particularly beneficial for older adults who want to enjoy fried foods with less oil, reducing health concerns associated with excess fat intake.

• Crispier Reheating: Air fryers are excellent for reheating leftovers. They can make reheated foods crispy and enjoyable, unlike microwaves that often make leftovers soggy.

While these advantages may not be as popular as the more well-known benefits of air fryers, they contribute to making air fryers a useful addition to your kitchen.

Why are air fryers so popular?

Air fryers are becoming increasingly popular and for a good reason. I would recommend them. But why? Well, they offer several advantages over traditional cooking methods, including:

• Healthier cooking: Air fryers use hot air to

circulate food, cooking it evenly without needing a lot of oil. This means that air-fried foods are typically lower in calories and fat than deep-fried foods, improving your health!

- Versatility: Air fryers can cook various foods, from chicken nuggets and french fries to vegetables and seafood. They can also be used to reheat leftovers and cook frozen foods.
- Convenience: Air fryers are easy to use and clean. Place your food in the basket, set the timer and temperature, and let the air fryer do the rest.
- Safety: Air fryers are safer than deep fryers because there is no risk of hot oil splattering.
- Faster cooking time: Air fryers can cook food faster than traditional ovens, making them an excellent option for busy weeknights.
- Less mess: Air fryers are less messy than other cooking methods, such as deep frying or stovetop cooking.
- Energy efficiency: Air fryers use less energy than traditional ovens. This can save you money on your utility bills.

Overall, air fryers are a convenient and healthy way to cook various foods. If you are looking for a new kitchen appliance, I'd recommend an air fryer.

Chapter 2: All about Ninja Air Fryers

Ninja Air Fryers are the best in the market at the moment. They have garnered thousands of positive reviews and user feedback on selling platforms. Based on personal experience as well, they are worth the hype.

I have made a pick of their top 5 models you can consider. They include:

Ninja DZ201 and DZ401 models

At first glance, these two models appear nearly identical. However, a closer examination of their technical specifications reveals a significant difference that can help you choose the best suits your requirements. Ninja currently produces the finest dual-basket air fryers for several compelling reasons.

Ninja DZ201 Model

With over 15,000 Amazon reviews, the Ninja DZ201 emerges as a highly sought-after air fryer. If you're looking for a versatile and user-friendly kitchen appliance, this is definitely for you.

But why? It has an impressive 90% 5-star rating. This is a high degree of satisfaction among its users.

A standout feature of the DZ201 is its Dual Zone Technology. This feature is also present in the DZ401 model. This innovative design incorporates two baskets, significantly expanding its cooking capacity.

What sets it apart further is the introduction of Smart Finish, a functionality that enables you to simultaneously prepare two different dishes, ensuring they complete their cooking cycles simultaneously.

Moreover, the Match Cook feature simplifies the process. I can now copy the settings of one basket to the other. How cool is that? This eliminates the need for manual input of temperature and time, which is handy if you've manually set these parameters instead of selecting a pre-set option.

Ninja DZ401 model

If you're in the market for the finest 10-quart air fryers, I'd recommend DZ401. While it is not as popular as the DZ201, it is a fantastic alternative, especially if you want a slightly larger option.

Thanks to its extensive temperature range, you can prepare various dishes and choose the precise setting to achieve your desired results. Its temperature range spans from 105 to 450 degrees Fahrenheit, just like the DZ201 model.

However, the DZ401 has IQ Boost, which differs from the DZ201. This feature ensures optimal power distribution across both baskets when you haven't selected Smart Finish or Match Cook.

It proves invaluable for maintaining consistent results when simultaneously cooking two dishes requiring different heat levels.

Ninja Air Fryer Max XL (AF161)

The Ninja Air fryerAF161 is another excellent cooking appliance I'd recommend. Experience the benefits of healthier cooking with up to 75% less fat compared to traditional frying methods.

Furthermore, up your cooking game with Max Crisp Technology, which delivers a searing 450 degrees of superheated air. This not only allows for cooking foods up to 30% faster than the Ninja AF100 but also results in hotter, crispier dishes.

Embrace the convenience of a spacious 5.5-quart ceramic-coated nonstick basket and crisper plate. This ample capacity accommodates up to 3 pounds of French fries or chicken wings. This is perfect for your family meals and gatherings.

Unleash your culinary creativity with seven cooking modes at your disposal. These include Max Crisp, Air Fry, Air Roast, Air Broil, Bake, Reheat, and Dehydrate. All these help you ensure you can prepare a wide range of delicious dishes. Say goodbye to the hassle of scrubbing and soaking, as it's effortless to clean.

Ninja Foodi Digital Air Fry Oven (FT102CO)

The Ninja Foodi Digital FT102CO is the ultimate kitchen appliance! Imagine a meal-making the power to air fry, air roast, air broil, bake, make bagels, toast, dehydrate, and keep your food warm.

Reclaim your countertop space by storing it neatly against your backsplash, taking up 50% less space. Enjoy healthier cooking with up to 75% less fat than traditional frying methods, as tested against deep-fried hand-cut French fries.

Its extra-large capacity offers 45% more cooking area than the Cuisinart toa-60 and toa-65 pans. It can accommodate a 13" pizza, up to 9 slices of toast, or six chicken breasts (6-8 oz. each). Cleaning is a breeze with a removable crumb tray and an easily accessible back panel for deep cleaning.

Experience fast cooking, up to 60% quicker than a standard oven with air roast, thanks to its 60-second preheat and the ability to prepare full

meals in as little as 20 minutes. Its digital crisp control technology ensures precision-controlled temperature, heat source, and airflow for versatile and optimal cooking performance.

Ninja Air Fryer (AF101)

With Ninja Air Fryer (AF101), now savour guilt-free meals with up to a 75% reduction in fat compared to traditional frying methods. It also allows you to tweak your cooking settings as you desire.

Achieve gentle moisture removal or quick cooking and crisping with convection heat, ranging from 105°F to 400°F. The 4-quart ceramic-coated nonstick basket and crisper plate can accommodate up to 2 lbs of French fries. Family meals are no longer a problem!

It's equipped with four versatile cooking modes, including Air Fry, Roast, Reheat, and Dehydrate. Enjoy craft flat, chip-like dehydrated snacks with various dehydration options. The combination of low fan speed and low temperature ensures thorough dehydration. Furthermore, parts, including the basket and crisper plate, are dishwasher-safe. Simply wipe the machine's exterior to keep it clean.

Ninja Foodi 10-in-1 XL Pro Air Fry Oven (DT251)

Experience up to 10 times the convection power compared to a traditional full-size convection oven, ensuring faster, crispier, and juicier results. Cook better meals harnessing its ten modes, including Air Fry, Air Roast, Bake, Whole Roast, Broil, Toast, Bagel, Dehydrate, Reheat, and Pizza.

Achieve the perfect level of doneness, from

rare to well done, with ease using the integrated Foodi Smart Thermometer. This saves you from guessing.

With a 90-second oven preheat time and up to 30% faster cooking than a traditional full-size convection oven, you can prepare meals quickly. Cook efficiently on two levels without the need for rotation. It can accommodate a 5-lb chicken and a sheet pan of vegetables, two 12-inch pizzas, or a 12-lb turkey. Prepare two sheet pan meals simultaneously for entertaining or weekly meal preparation.

Enjoy healthier air fryer options & crisp results; use the Air Fry function to enjoy meals with up to 75% less fat than traditional deep frying (tested against hand-cut, deep-fried French fries). Get up to 30% crispier outcomes compared to a conventional convection oven.

The selected function illuminates the optimal oven rack positions, and the display settings remain locked when the door is open to prevent accidental changes during cooking. Experience up to 50% more consistent baking results than a leading countertop oven.

Why Choose the Ninja Dual Zone?

The Ninja Air Fryer is an excellent appliance, one I'd recommend you add to your Kitchen. It can definitely save you a lot of stress and make your cooking faster, better and healthier. Here are some reasons to choose the Ninja Dual Zone Air Fryer:

- Powerful Convection: The Ninja Dual Zone Air Fryer boasts true surround convection technology, providing up to 10 times the convection power compared to traditional full-size convection ovens. This means faster, crispier, and juicier results.

- Versatile Cooking: With up to 10 cooking modes in one appliance, you can air fry, roast, bake, whole roast, broil, toast, make bagels, dehydrate, reheat, and even cook pizza. It's a kitchen workhorse that can handle various cooking tasks.

- Precision Cooking: The integrated Foodi Smart Thermometer ensures perfect doneness at the touch of a button, eliminating guesswork and helping you achieve your desired level of cooking from rare to well done.

- Time-Saving: Dual zone air fryers offer quick family meals with a 90-second oven preheat time. It is up to 30% faster cooking than traditional full-size convection ovens. This is especially useful for busy households.

- Extra-Large Capacity: The appliance provides 2-level cooking without the need for rotation. It can accommodate large meals, such as a 5-lb chicken with a sheet pan of vegetables, two 12-inch pizzas, or even a 12-lb turkey. Perfect for larger gatherings or meal prepping.

- Healthier Cooking: Enjoy healthier meals with the Air Fry function, which can reduce fat by up to 75% compared to traditional deep frying, tested against hand-cut, deep-fried French fries. Plus, it delivers up to 30% crispier results compared to a standard convection oven.

- User-Friendly: The digital display handle makes it easy to select functions, and the oven rack positions illuminate based on your choice. The settings remain secure when the door is open, preventing accidental changes.

- Effortless for Entertaining: You can prepare two sheet pan meals simultaneously. It's perfect for hosting gatherings or simplifying your weekly meal preparation.

How to Use the Ninja Air Fryer

Using a Ninja Air Fryer is relatively straightforward. Here's a basic guide:

- Read the Manual: Start by reading the user manual that comes with your Ninja Air Fryer. This will provide specific instructions and safety guidelines for your particular model.

- Preparation: Place the air fryer on a clean, flat, and heat-resistant surface. Ensure there's

enough space around the air fryer for proper ventilation.

- Preheat the Air Fryer (if required): Some recipes may recommend preheating the air fryer. If so, set the desired temperature and let it preheat for a few minutes.
- Prepare Your Ingredients: Season or marinate your food as desired. Place your ingredients in a suitable container or air fryer basket/tray. Ensure they are in a single layer for even cooking.
- Select the Function: Choose the cooking function that best suits your dish. Ninja Air Fryers typically offer a variety of functions like Air Fry, Roast, Bake, etc. Use the control panel to select the appropriate function.
- Set the Time and Temperature: Use the control panel to set the cooking time and temperature. Refer to your recipe or the air fryer's guidelines for the recommended settings.
- Start Cooking: Press the start button to begin the cooking process.
- Check and Shake (if needed): Depending on your recipe, you may need to pause the cooking process to shake or flip your food for even results. Some air fryers even have a reminder to do this.
- Monitor Progress: Keep an eye on your food as it cooks. You can usually observe the cooking progress through the air fryer's transparent door or lid.
- Finish and Serve: When the cooking time is complete, carefully open the air fryer. Be cautious, as it will be hot. Use oven mitts or a towel to remove the food and place it on a serving plate.
- Let it Cool: Allow the air fryer to cool down before cleaning it.
- Cleaning: After each use, clean the air fryer's removable parts like the basket, tray, and crumb tray. Many parts are dishwasher-safe for convenience. Read on for tips on how to clean your Ninja Air Fryer.
- Storage: Once cleaned and completely cooled, store the air fryer in a safe and dry location.

Remember to refer to your specific Ninja Air Fryer's manual for model-specific instructions and safety precautions. Furthermore, always

follow the recommended cooking times and temperatures for your recipes to ensure the best results.

Tips and Tricks for Using the Ninja Air Fryer

Based on my experience with Ninja Air Fryer, I'd like to share some pro tips and tricks with you to give you a head start with the Ninja Air Fryer. They include:

- Use the Match Cook feature to cook different foods at different temperatures. This is an excellent feature for cooking a meal for everyone in your family, especially if they have different dietary restrictions.
- Use the Smart Finish feature to finish cooking two different foods at the same time. You can cook the main course and side dish together.
- If you're cooking multiple batches of food, preheat the air fryer between batches. This will help to ensure that all of your food cooks evenly.
- Don't overcrowd the air fryer baskets. Overcrowding might prevent the hot air from circulating freely and can result in uneven cooking.
- Shake or toss the food halfway through cooking. This will help to ensure that the food cooks evenly.
- Use a little bit of oil on your food. Slight oiling might be necessary to prevent the food from sticking to the air fryer baskets.
- Be careful when removing the food from the air fryer baskets. The baskets will be hot.
- Clean the air fryer baskets after each use. This will help to prevent the build-up of food and grease.
- Use parchment paper or a silicone baking mat in the air fryer baskets. This will help to

prevent food from sticking and make cleanup easier.

- If you're cooking breaded foods, spray the breading with a little bit of oil before air frying for breading crispy.
- If you're cooking frozen foods, there is no need to thaw them before air frying. Simply place the frozen food in the air fryer basket and cook according to the package directions.
- To make your own air fryer croutons, cut bread into cubes and toss with some olive oil and seasonings. Air fry at 350 degrees Fahrenheit for 5-7 minutes or until the croutons are golden brown and crispy.
- To make your own air fryer popcorn, place a single layer of popcorn kernels in the air fryer basket. Air fry at 400 degrees Fahrenheit for 2-3 minutes, or until the popcorn is popped.

With a bit of practice, you'll be air-frying like a pro in no time!

Cleaning and Maintenance

Cleaning your Air Fryer is very important to ensure efficiency and longevity. I'd like to share my cleaning tips with you below:

- Unplug the air fryer and let it cool completely.
- Remove the air fryer basket and crisper tray. You can wash these parts by hand or in the dishwasher.
- Wipe the inside and outside of the air fryer with a damp cloth. Be careful not to get water into the electrical components of the air fryer.
- If there is any stubborn grease or food residue, you can use a mild dish soap and water solution to clean it. Be sure to rinse the air fryer thoroughly with clean water after cleaning.
- Dry the air fryer completely before using it again.
- Clean the air fryer basket and crisper tray after each use. This will help to prevent the build-up of food and grease.
- If you're not using the air fryer basket or crisper tray, you can soak them in warm, soapy water for a few minutes before cleaning. This will help to loosen any stuck-on food.
- You can use a mild dish soap and water solution to clean the inside and outside of the air fryer. Be sure to rinse the air fryer thoroughly with clean water after cleaning.
- If there is any stubborn grease or food residue on the inside of the air fryer, you can use a baking soda paste to clean it.
- Make a paste with baking soda and water and apply it to the affected area. Let the paste sit for a few minutes before scrubbing it off with a damp cloth.
- To clean the heating element, use a soft brush to remove any food particles or grease. Be careful not to use any abrasive cleaners or scrubbers, as this could damage the heating element.
- With a bit of care and attention, your Ninja Air Fryer will stay clean and in good condition for many years to come.

Chapter 1 Breakfast

Popovers

Prep Time: 10 minutes / Cook Time: 30 minutes / Servings: 4

Ingredients:
- 150g all-purpose flour
- 2 large eggs
- 150ml milk
- 5g salt
- 5ml vegetable oil

Preparation Instructions:
1. Preheat the Ninja Air Fryer to 375°F using the Air Fry mode.
2. In a mixing bowl, combine the flour and salt.
3. In a separate bowl, whisk the eggs and milk together.
4. Gradually add the wet Ingredients to the dry ingredients, mixing until you have a smooth batter.
5. Brush each cup of a popover pan with vegetable oil.
6. Pour the batter into each cup, filling them halfway.
7. Place the popover pan in the air fryer basket.
8. Air fry for about 30 minutes until the popovers are golden brown and puffed up.
9. Remove from the air fryer, let them cool slightly, and serve immediately.

Grits

Prep Time: 5 minutes / Cook Time: 20 minutes / Servings: 4

Ingredients:
- 150g grits
- 600ml water
- 5g salt
- 15ml butter

Preparation Instructions:
1. Preheat the Ninja Air Fryer to 375°F using the Air Fry mode.
2. In a saucepan, bring the water to a boil. Add salt.
3. Gradually whisk in the grits, stirring constantly.
4. Reduce the heat to low, cover, and simmer for about 15-20 minutes, or until the grits are thick and creamy.
5. Stir in the butter until melted.
6. Spoon the grits into a serving dish.
7. Place the dish in the air fryer basket.
8. Air fry for about 5 minutes to give the top a nice golden crust.
9. Remove from the air fryer and let it cool slightly before serving.

Polenta

Prep Time: 10 minutes / Cook Time: 25 minutes / Servings: 4

Ingredients:
- 150g polenta
- 600ml water
- 5g salt
- 30ml butter
- 30g grated parmesan cheese

Preparation Instructions:
1. Preheat the Ninja Air Fryer to 375°F using the Bake mode.
2. In a saucepan, bring the water to a boil. Add salt.
3. Gradually whisk in the polenta, stirring constantly.
4. Reduce the heat to low, cover, and simmer for about 20-25 minutes, or until the polenta is thick and creamy.
5. Stir in the butter and grated parmesan cheese until well incorporated.
6. Transfer the polenta to a serving dish.
7. Place the dish in the air fryer basket.
8. Bake for about 5 minutes to give the top a nice golden crust.
9. Remove from the air fryer and let it cool slightly before serving.

Omelette Arnold Bennett

Prep Time: 10 minutes / Cook Time: 15 minutes / Servings: 2

Ingredients:
- 4 large eggs
- 150g smoked haddock, cooked and flaked
- 30ml hollandaise sauce
- Salt and pepper to taste
- 10g grated cheddar cheese

Preparation Instructions:
1. Preheat the Ninja Air Fryer to 375°F using the Roast mode.
2. In a bowl, whisk the eggs and season with salt and pepper.
3. Add the flaked smoked haddock to the eggs and mix well.

4. Grease an ovenproof dish with a bit of oil or butter.
5. Pour the egg and haddock mixture into the dish.
6. Roast for about 15 minutes, or until the omelette is set and slightly puffed up.
7. Remove from the air fryer and drizzle hollandaise sauce over the omelette.
8. Sprinkle grated cheddar cheese on top.
9. Roast for an additional 2-3 minutes until the cheese is melted and bubbly.
10. Serve the Omelette Arnold Bennett hot and enjoy with family.

Nachos

Prep Time: 10 minutes / Cook Time: 8 minutes / Servings: 4

Ingredients:
- 200g tortilla chips
- 150g shredded cheddar cheese
- 100g black beans, drained and rinsed
- 100g diced tomatoes
- 50g sliced jalapeños (adjust to your spice preference)
- 50g diced red onion
- 50g sliced black olives

Preparation Instructions:
1. Preheat the Ninja Air Fryer to 375°F using the Air Fry mode.
2. Arrange half of the tortilla chips in the air fryer basket.
3. Sprinkle half of the cheddar cheese over the chips.
4. Add half of the black beans, diced tomatoes, jalapeños, red onion, and black olives.
5. Repeat the layering with the remaining half of the ingredients.
6. Air fry for about 8 minutes or until the cheese is melted and the nachos are heated through.
7. Carefully remove and serve immediately with your favorite toppings and dips.

Strata

Prep Time: 15 minutes / Cook Time: 35 minutes / Servings: 6

Ingredients:
- 300g bread cubes
- 200ml milk
- 4 large eggs
- 150g shredded cheddar cheese
- 100g diced ham
- 50g sliced green onions
- 5g salt
- 2. 5g black pepper

Preparation Instructions:
1. Preheat the Ninja Air Fryer to 375°F using the Bake mode.
2. In a mixing bowl, whisk together the milk, eggs, salt, and black pepper.
3. In a separate bowl, combine the bread cubes, diced ham, shredded cheddar cheese, and sliced green onions.
4. Pour the egg mixture over the bread mixture and gently toss to coat.
5. Transfer the mixture to a greased ovenproof dish.
6. Place the dish in the air fryer basket.
7. Bake for about 35 minutes or until the strata is set and golden brown.
8. Allow it to cool slightly before serving.

Taquitos

Prep Time: 15 minutes / Cook Time: 12 minutes / Servings: 4

Ingredients:
- 200g shredded chicken
- 100g cream cheese
- 50g shredded cheddar cheese
- 50g diced green Chillies
- 1g taco seasoning
- 8 small corn tortillas
- Cooking spray

Preparation Instructions:
1. Preheat the Ninja Air Fryer to 375°F using the Air Fry mode.
2. In a bowl, combine the shredded chicken, cream cheese, shredded cheddar cheese, diced green Chillies, and taco seasoning.
3. Warm the corn tortillas in the microwave for about 30 seconds to make them pliable.
4. Place a spoonful of the chicken mixture in the centre of each tortilla.
5. Roll up the tortillas tightly and secure with toothpicks.
6. Lightly spray the taquitos with cooking spray.
7. Air fry for about 12 minutes, turning them halfway through, until they are crispy and golden.
8. Remove the toothpicks and serve with your favourite dipping sauce.

Breakfast Calzones

Prep Time: 15 minutes / Cook Time: 12 minutes / Servings: 4

Ingredients:
- 200g pizza dough
- 4 large eggs

- 100g cooked breakfast sausage, crumbled
- 100g shredded cheddar cheese
- 50g diced bell peppers
- Salt and pepper to taste

Preparation Instructions:

1. Preheat the Ninja Air Fryer to 375°F using the Air Fry mode.
2. Divide the pizza dough into four equal portions.
3. Roll out each portion of dough into a circle.
4. In a bowl, beat one egg and season with salt and pepper.
5. Place a portion of the cooked breakfast sausage, shredded cheddar cheese, and diced bell peppers on one half of each dough circle.
6. Fold the other half of the dough over to cover the fillings, forming a half-moon shape.
7. Seal the edges by pressing with a fork.
8. Brush the top of each calzone with the beaten egg.
9. Air fry for about 12 minutes or until the calzones are golden and the egg is set.
10. Allow them to cool slightly before serving.

Tostadas

Prep Time: 10 minutes / Cook Time: 5 minutes / Servings: 4

Ingredients:

- 4 small corn tortillas
- 200g refried beans
- 100g shredded lettuce
- 100g diced tomatoes
- 50g diced red onion
- 50g sliced black olives
- 30g shredded cheddar cheese

Preparation Instructions:

1. Preheat the Ninja Air Fryer to 375°F using the Air Fry mode.
2. Place the corn tortillas in the air fryer basket.
3. Air fry for about 5 minutes or until they are crispy and lightly browned.
4. Remove the tortillas from the air fryer.
5. Spread refried beans on each tostada shell.
6. Top with shredded lettuce, diced tomatoes, diced red onion, sliced black olives, and shredded cheddar cheese.
7. Serve your tostadas with your favorite toppings and sauces.

Pot Pies

Prep Time: 20 minutes / Cook Time: 20 minutes / Servings: 4

Ingredients:

- 200g cooked chicken, diced

- 200g mixed vegetables (peas, carrots, corn)
- 200ml chicken gravy
- 200g refrigerated pie dough
- Salt and pepper to taste

Preparation Instructions:

1. Preheat the Ninja Air Fryer to 375°F using the Bake mode.
2. In a bowl, combine the cooked chicken, mixed vegetables, and chicken gravy. Season with salt and pepper.
3. Roll out the refrigerated pie dough and cut it into four circles, slightly larger than your ramekins.
4. Fill each ramekin with the chicken and vegetable mixture.
5. Place a circle of pie dough on top of each ramekin to create a lid. Press the edges to seal.
6. Cut a small slit in the centre of each pie for venting.
7. Place the ramekins in the air fryer basket.
8. Bake for about 20 minutes or until the pot pies are golden brown and the filling is bubbling.
9. Let them cool slightly before serving.

Hogs Pudding

Prep Time: 10 minutes / Cook Time: 25 minutes / Servings: 4

Ingredients:

- 200g hog pudding (sausage)
- 150g potatoes, peeled and diced
- 100g onions, chopped
- 50ml vegetable oil
- Salt and pepper to taste

Preparation Instructions:

1. Preheat the Ninja Air Fryer to 375°F using the Roast mode.
2. In a mixing bowl, combine the diced potatoes, chopped onions, vegetable oil, salt, and pepper. Toss to coat.
3. Place the seasoned potatoes and onions in the air fryer basket.
4. Add the hog pudding on top.
5. Roast for about 25 minutes or until the hog pudding is cooked through and the potatoes are golden and crispy.
6. Remove from the air fryer and serve.

Eggs Royale

Prep Time: 15 minutes / Cook Time: 10 minutes / Servings: 2

Ingredients:

- 2 English muffins, split
- 4 large eggs

- 150g smoked salmon
- 100ml hollandaise sauce

Preparation Instructions:

1. Preheat the Ninja Air Fryer to 375°F using the Air Fry mode.
2. Place the English muffin halves in the air fryer basket, cut side up.
3. Air fry for about 5 minutes or until they are toasted and slightly crispy.
4. Remove the toasted muffins from the air fryer.
5. Poach the eggs using your preferred method.
6. Place the toasted English muffin halves on a serving plate.
7. Top each half with smoked salmon and a poached egg.
8. Drizzle hollandaise sauce over the eggs.
9. Serve your hot and enjoy your delicious breakfast meal.

Soldiers and Eggs

Prep Time: 10 minutes / Cook Time: 5 minutes / Servings: 2

Ingredients:

- 2 large eggs
- 4 slices of bread
- 30g butter, softened
- Salt and pepper to taste

Preparation Instructions:

1. Preheat the Ninja Air Fryer to 375°F using the Air Fry mode.
2. Spread the softened butter on the bread slices.
3. Cut the bread into "soldiers" by slicing them into strips.
4. Place the bread soldiers in the air fryer basket.
5. Air fry for about 5 minutes or until they are golden and crispy.
6. While the soldiers are cooking, prepare soft-boiled eggs according to your preference.
7. Season the eggs with salt and pepper.
8. Serve the crispy soldiers with the soft-boiled eggs for dipping.

English Breakfast Pie

Prep Time: 20 minutes / Cook Time: 30 minutes / Servings: 4

Ingredients:

- 200g puff pastry
- 4 large eggs
- 100g cooked bacon, chopped
- 100g cooked sausages, sliced
- 100g baked beans

- 50g sliced mushrooms
- Salt and pepper to taste

Preparation Instructions:

1. Preheat the Ninja Air Fryer to 375°F using the Bake mode.
2. Roll out the puff pastry and line a pie dish.
3. Layer the cooked bacon, sliced sausages, baked beans, and sliced mushrooms in the pie dish.
4. Crack the eggs on top of the mixture.
5. Season with salt and pepper.
6. Cover the pie with another layer of puff pastry and seal the edges.
7. Cut a small slit in the centre for venting.
8. Place the pie in the air fryer basket.
9. Bake for about 30 minutes or until the pastry is golden brown and the eggs are set.
10. Allow it to cool slightly before serving.

Omelette Norvégienne

Prep Time: 15 minutes / Cook Time: 5 minutes / Servings: 2

Ingredients:

- 2 large eggs
- 100g smoked salmon
- 100g cream cheese
- 50g sugar
- 50g water
- 20g granulated sugar

Preparation Instructions:

1. Preheat the Ninja Air Fryer to 375°F using the Air Fry mode.
2. In a bowl, beat the eggs until frothy.
3. Pour the beaten eggs into an ovenproof dish.
4. Air fry for about 5 minutes or until the omelette is set.
5. While the omelette is cooking, prepare a simple syrup by combining sugar and water in a saucepan. Bring it to a boil and let it cool.
6. Remove the omelette from the air fryer.
7. Spread cream cheese on top of the omelette.
8. Roll up the omelette with the cream cheese inside.
9. Drizzle the simple syrup over the rolled omelette.
10. Use a culinary torch to lightly brown the top.
11. Serve while hot for the best taste.

Derbyshire Oatcakes

Prep Time: 15 minutes / Cook Time: 10 minutes / Servings: 4

Ingredients:

- 200g oat flour
- 150ml milk

- 2 large eggs
- 5g salt
- 30g butter

Preparation Instructions:

1. Preheat the Ninja Air Fryer to 375°F using the Air Fry mode.
2. In a mixing bowl, combine the oat flour and salt.
3. In a separate bowl, whisk together the milk and eggs.
4. Gradually add the wet Ingredients to the dry ingredients, mixing until you have a smooth batter.
5. Melt the butter in a small saucepan.
6. Add the melted butter to the batter and mix well.
7. Pour a ladleful of the batter into the air fryer basket and spread it out to create a thin oatcake.
8. Air fry for about 5-7 minutes, flipping halfway through, until the oatcake is golden and crispy.
9. Repeat with the remaining batter.
10. Serve your Derbyshire Oatcakes with your favorite toppings.

Staffordshire Griddle Cakes

Prep Time: 10 minutes / Cook Time: 10 minutes / Servings: 4

Ingredients:

- 200g all-purpose flour
- 5g baking powder
- 30g sugar
- 50g butter
- 150ml milk

Preparation Instructions:

1. Preheat the Ninja Air Fryer to 375°F using the Air Fry mode.
2. In a mixing bowl, combine the all-purpose flour, baking powder, and sugar.
3. Add the butter to the dry Ingredients and rub it in until the mixture resembles breadcrumbs.
4. Gradually add the milk, mixing until you have a soft dough.
5. Roll out the dough on a floured surface to about 1/2 inch thickness.
6. Use a cookie cutter to cut out griddle cakes.
7. Place the griddle cakes in the air fryer basket.
8. Air fry for about 8-10 minutes, turning halfway through, until the griddle cakes are golden brown.
9. Serve your Staffordshire Griddle Cakes warm for the best taste.

Stotties

Prep Time: 15 minutes / Cook Time: 10 minutes / Servings: 4

Ingredients:

- 300g strong white bread flour
- 5g salt
- 7g sugar
- 5g active dry yeast
- 200ml warm water
- 15ml vegetable oil

Preparation Instructions:

1. Preheat the Ninja Air Fryer to 375°F using the Air Fry mode.
2. In a mixing bowl, combine the strong white bread flour, salt, and sugar.
3. In a small bowl, dissolve the active dry yeast in warm water. Let it sit for about 5 minutes until frothy.
4. Make a well in the centre of the flour mixture and pour in the yeast mixture and vegetable oil.
5. Mix to form a soft dough.
6. Knead the dough on a floured surface for about 5 minutes until it's smooth and elastic.
7. Divide the dough into 4 equal portions and shape them into round, flat discs about 1 inch thick.
8. Place the stotties in the air fryer basket.
9. Air fry for about 10 minutes, or until they're golden and sound hollow when tapped on the bottom.
10. Remove from the air fryer and let them cool slightly.
11. Slice the stotties in half and fill them with your favorite ingredients, such as bacon, sausage, or other sandwich fillings.
12. Serve your Stotties as desired, with the fillings of your choice.

Devilled kidneys

Prep Time: 10-15 minutes / Cook Time: 15-20 minutes
Serves: 2-4

Ingredients:

- 4 lamb kidneys, halved and deveined
- 1 tablespoon plain flour
- 1 tablespoon English mustard powder
- 1 tablespoon Worcestershire sauce
- 1 tablespoon tomato ketchup
- 1 tablespoon butter
- Salt and freshly ground black pepper
- 2 slices of toasted bread, to serve

Preparation Instructions:

1. In a small bowl, mix the flour, mustard powder, Worcestershire sauce, and tomato ketchup to make a paste.
2. Preheat the Ninja Dual Zone to Air Fry at 200°C

3. Melt the butter in a frying pan over medium heat. Add the kidneys to the pan and season with salt and pepper. Cook for 2-3 minutes on each side until browned.
4. Add the flour paste to the pan and stir well to coat the kidneys. Cook for a further 1-2 minutes until the sauce has thickened.
5. Transfer the kidneys and sauce to the Ninja Dual Zone basket and cook for 8-10 minutes until the kidneys are cooked through and the sauce is bubbling.
6. Serve the devilled kidneys on toasted bread and enjoy!

Crispy Bacon and egg pie

Prep Time: 10 minutes / Cook Time: 15-20 minutes / Serves: 4

Ingredients:
- 1 sheet puff pastry, thawed
- 6 slices bacon, cooked until crispy and crumbled
- 4 eggs
- 118 ml of heavy cream
- Salt and freshly ground black pepper
- Chopped chives, to serve

Preparation Instructions:
1. Preheat the Ninja Dual Zone to Bake at 190°C (190°C).
2. Roll out the puff pastry on a lightly floured surface and transfer it to a 9-inch pie dish, trimming the edges as needed.
3. Sprinkle the crumbled bacon evenly over the bottom of the pie crust.
4. In a medium bowl, whisk together the eggs, heavy cream, salt, and black pepper.
5. Pour the egg mixture into the pie crust, covering the bacon.
6. Bake the pie in the Ninja Dual for 20 minutes, or until the crust is golden brown and the eggs are set.
7. Remove the pie from the Ninja Dual and let it cool for a few minutes before slicing.
8. Sprinkle with chopped chives and serve hot.

Breakfast Brownies

Prep Time: 10 minutes / Cook time: 40 minutes / Serves 8

Ingredients:
- 200g quick oats
- 50g brown sugar
- 1 tbsp cocoa powder
- 1 tbsp flaxseed meal
- 1/4 tsp cinnamon powder
- 120ml unsweetened applesauce
- 1 egg, beaten
- 350ml coconut milk
- 40g dark chocolate chunks

Preparation Instructionss:
1. Remove a crisper plate from your Nina Foodi. Line the zone 1 and 2 drawers with a piece of baking paper.
2. In a mixing bowl, thoroughly combine the oats, sugar, cocoa powder, flaxseed meal, and cinnamon powder.
3. Then, gradually and slowly, stir in the applesauce, egg, and coconut milk; mix until creamy and uniform. Fold in the chocolate chunks and whisk to combine well.
4. Spoon the batter into the prepared drawers.
5. Select zone 1 and pair it with "BAKE" at 160°C for 40 minutes. Select "MATCH" followed by the "START/STOP" button.
6. Check your brownies with a toothpick; allow your brownies to rest on a cooling rack for about 10 minutes before cutting and serving.

Star Anise Muffins

Prep Time: 10 minutes / Cook time: 15 minutes / Serves 8

Ingredients
- 2 large eggs
- 300g apple sauce
- 200g brown sugar
- 100g coconut oil
- 200g self-raising plain flour
- A pinch of sea salt
- 1/4 tsp ground anise
- 1/4 tsp ground cinnam

Preparation Instructions:
1. Remove a crisper plate from your Ninja Foodi. Preheat the Ninja Foodi to 160°C for 5 minutes. Spray 8 muffin cases with nonstick oil.
2. In a separate mixing bowl, whisk the eggs until pale and frothy. Slowly and gradually, stir in apple sauce, brown sugar, and coconut oil; mix until everything is well incorporated.
3. In another bowl, thoroughly combine the dry ingredients.
4. Slowly and gradually, add the dry Ingredients to the wet ingredients; mix again to combine. Spoon the batter into the prepared muffin cases. Place 4 muffin cases in each drawer.
5. Select zone 1 and pair it with "BAKE" at 160°C for 15 minutes. Select "MATCH" followed by the "START/STOP" button.

6. Allow your muffins to rest on a cooling rack for about 10 minutes before unmolding and serving.

Air Fryer Breakfast Burritos

Prep Time: 20 mins / Cook Time: 10 mins / Servings: 2

Ingredients

- Ground Chicken
- Ground Sausage
- 1 Diced Potatoes (Red or Yellowish)
- 1 large Yellow, Red and Green Bell Peppers, all diced
- 28g of Shredded Cheese
- ½ Onions bulb, Red and Sweet cut in rings
- 2 Eggs
- Olive Oil
- ⅛ tablespoon of Black Pepper
- Salt to taste
- 2 tbsp Butter
- Garlic Powder
- Tortillas (10-inch sized)
- Salsa or Sour Cream

Preparation Instructions:

1. Preheat the Ninja Dual Zone Air Fryer to 350°F (175°C).
2. While you preheat the Air Fryer, melt 2 tablespoonfuls of butter in 3 tablespoonfuls of olive oil separately in a saucepan over medium heat.
3. Add in the diced potatoes, stir and cook for 7-8 mins, then add the onion rings and diced peppers.
4. Saute this for 4 minutes more, then remove it from heat and set it aside.
5. Cook the ground chicken and sausage with spices to your taste, drain and set it aside.
6. In a bowl, beat eggs and season with salt and pepper.
7. Heat a frying pan over medium heat and scramble the eggs until cooked.
8. Place a tortilla on a flat surface and add a spoonful of scrambled eggs, cooked sausage and chicken, sauteed potatoes, shredded cheese, and any other desired fillings.
9. Fold the sides of the tortilla inward and roll it tightly.
10. Lightly spray the burrito with cooking spray and place it seam-side down in the Ninja Dual Zone Air Fryer drawers.
11. Cook for 8-10 minutes until the tortilla is crispy and golden. Serve with salsa or sour cream.

Air Fryer Egg Cups

Prep Time: 3 mins / Cook Time: 12 mins / Servings: 2

Ingredients

- 2 large sized Eggs
- Salt and Pepper as preferred
- 40g Ham or Bacon
- Shredded Cheese
- ½ Onions bulb
- Mushrooms
- 3 Tbsp Milk (optional)
- Preferred spices

Preparation Instructions

1. Preheat the Ninja Dual Zone Air fryer to 325°F (165°C).
2. Spray muffin cups with cooking spray.
3. Dice up all the fillings, i. e. the ham or bacon, whichever you choose, the onions, mushrooms etc.
4. Line each cup with some ham or bacon.
5. Crack an egg into each cup, careful not to break the yolk. You can also choose to whisk the egg before you put it in. Take your pick.
6. Put in the mushrooms, onions and any other additional fillings you've chosen
7. Season with salt, pepper, and any desired herbs or spices.
8. Add the shredded cheese as toppings.
9. Place the muffin tin into your Ninja Dual Zone Air Fryer drawers.
10. Set it to cook for 8-10 minutes, or until the eggs are set to your liking.
11. Ensure the cheese is well melted and the cups are golden brown around the edges.
12. Press the egg cup down, and it's cooked enough when it bounces back to shape or is puffy.
13. Carefully remove the egg cups from the air fryer and serve hot.

Chapter 2 Beans and Grains

SourDough Boule

Prep Time: 15 minutes / Cook Time: 25 minutes / Servings: 1 boule

Ingredients:
- 250g all-purpose flour
- 150g active sourdough starter
- 150ml warm water
- 5g salt

Preparation Instructions:
1. Preheat the Ninja Air Fryer to 375°F using the Bake mode.
2. In a mixing bowl, combine the all-purpose flour and salt.
3. Add the active sourdough starter and warm water to the flour mixture.
4. Mix the Ingredients until a shaggy dough forms.
5. Turn the dough out onto a lightly floured surface and knead it for about 5 minutes until it becomes smooth and elastic.
6. Shape the dough into a boule (round loaf).
7. Place the boule in a lightly floured ovenproof dish or on a piece of parchment paper.
8. Score the top of the boule with a sharp knife to allow for expansion during baking.
9. Place the dish with the boule in the air fryer basket.
10. Bake for about 25 minutes or until the boule is golden brown and sounds hollow when tapped on the bottom.
11. Remove from the air fryer and let it cool on a wire rack.
12. Slice and enjoy your homemade Sourdough Boule.

Barley and Butternut Squash Risotto

Prep Time: 15 minutes / Cook Time: 30 minutes / Servings: 4

Ingredients:
- 200g pearl barley
- 400g butternut squash, diced
- 100g onion, chopped
- 1 liter vegetable broth
- 30g grated Parmesan cheese
- 30ml olive oil
- Salt and pepper to taste

Preparation Instructions:
1. Preheat the Ninja Air Fryer to 375°F using the Bake mode.
2. In a baking dish, combine the pearl barley, diced butternut squash, chopped onion, and olive oil.
3. Roast for about 30 minutes or until the butternut squash is tender and the barley is slightly toasted.
4. Remove the baking dish from the air fryer.
5. Transfer the roasted mixture to a large saucepan.
6. Add the vegetable broth, a little at a time, and cook the barley until it's tender and creamy, stirring frequently.
7. Stir in the grated Parmesan cheese and season with salt and pepper.
8. Serve your Barley and Butternut Squash Risotto hot.

Barley and Spinach Soup

Prep Time: 10 minutes / Cook Time: 25 minutes / Servings: 4

Ingredients:
- 150g pearl barley
- 200g fresh spinach
- 100g carrots, diced
- 100g onions, chopped
- 1 liter vegetable broth
- 30ml olive oil
- Salt and pepper to taste

Preparation Instructions:
1. Preheat the Ninja Air Fryer to 375°F using the Bake mode.
2. In a baking dish, combine the pearl barley, diced carrots, chopped onions, and olive oil.
3. Roast for about 20 minutes or until the vegetables are tender and the barley is slightly toasted.
4. Remove the baking dish from the air fryer.
5. Transfer the roasted mixture to a large saucepan.
6. Add the vegetable broth and bring to a simmer.
7. Stir in the fresh spinach and cook until wilted.
8. Season with salt and pepper.
9. Serve hot and enjoy.

Lentil and Potato Bake

Prep Time: 15 minutes / Cook Time: 40 minutes / Servings: 4

Ingredients:
- 200g brown or green lentils
- 400g potatoes, thinly sliced
- 100g onions, chopped

- 100g carrots, sliced
- 1 can (400g) diced tomatoes
- 200ml vegetable broth
- 5g garlic powder
- 5g dried thyme
- Salt and pepper to taste

Preparation Instructions:

1. Preheat the Ninja Air Fryer to 375°F using the Bake mode.
2. In a baking dish, layer the thinly sliced potatoes, chopped onions, and sliced carrots.
3. Rinse and drain the lentils, then sprinkle them over the vegetables.
4. In a separate bowl, combine the diced tomatoes, vegetable broth, garlic powder, dried thyme, salt, and pepper.
5. Pour the tomato mixture over the vegetables and lentils.
6. Cover the baking dish with foil.
7. Place the dish in the air fryer basket.
8. Bake for about 40 minutes or until the lentils are tender and the potatoes are cooked through.
9. Remove from the air fryer and let it cool slightly before serving.

Bean and Parsnip Casserole

Prep Time: 15 minutes / Cook Time: 40 minutes / Servings: 4

Ingredients:

- 400g parsnips, sliced
- 400g canned mixed beans
- 100g onions, chopped
- 200ml vegetable broth
- 5g dried rosemary
- 5g garlic powder
- Salt and pepper to taste

Preparation Instructions:

1. Preheat the Ninja Air Fryer to 375°F using the Bake mode.
2. In a baking dish, combine the sliced parsnips, chopped onions, and canned mixed beans.
3. In a separate bowl, mix the vegetable broth, dried rosemary, garlic powder, salt, and pepper.
4. Pour the broth mixture over the vegetables and beans.
5. Cover the baking dish with foil.
6. Place the dish in the air fryer basket.
7. Bake for about 40 minutes or until the parsnips are tender and the casserole is hot and bubbly.
8. Remove from the air fryer and let it cool slightly before serving.

Red Lentil and Tomato Dahl

Prep Time: 15 minutes / Cook Time: 25 minutes / Servings: 4

Ingredients:

- 200g red lentils
- 400ml canned tomatoes
- 100g onions, chopped
- 5g ground cumin
- 5g ground coriander
- 5g turmeric
- 5g paprika
- Salt and pepper to taste

Preparation Instructions:

1. Preheat the Ninja Air Fryer to 375°F using the Bake mode.
2. In a baking dish, combine the red lentils, chopped onions, canned tomatoes, ground cumin, ground coriander, turmeric, paprika, salt, and pepper.
3. Mix everything together.
4. Cover the baking dish with foil.
5. Place the dish in the air fryer basket.
6. Bake for about 25 minutes or until the lentils are soft and the dahl is heated through.
7. Remove from the air fryer and let it cool slightly before serving.

Rice and Bean Enchiladas

Prep Time: 20 minutes / Cook Time: 25 minutes / Servings: 4

Ingredients:

- 200g cooked rice
- 200g canned black beans
- 200g canned red enchilada sauce
- 100g diced bell peppers
- 100g diced onions
- 100g shredded cheddar cheese
- 4 large tortillas

Preparation Instructions:

1. Preheat the Ninja Air Fryer to 375°F using the Bake mode.
2. In a mixing bowl, combine the cooked rice, black beans, diced bell peppers, and diced onions.
3. Lay out a tortilla and spoon some of the rice and bean mixture down the centre. Roll up the tortilla and place it seam side down in a baking dish.
4. Repeat with the remaining tortillas.
5. Pour the red enchilada sauce over the enchiladas.
6. Sprinkle shredded cheddar cheese on top.
7. Cover the baking dish with foil.
8. Place the dish in the air fryer basket.

9. Bake for about 25 minutes or until the enchiladas are hot and the cheese is melted.
10. Remove from the air fryer and let them cool slightly before serving.

Chickpea and Carrot Tagine

Prep Time: 15 minutes / Cook Time: 30 minutes / Servings: 4

Ingredients:
- 200g chickpeas, cooked
- 300g carrots, sliced
- 100g onions, chopped
- 100g canned diced tomatoes
- 100ml vegetable broth
- 5g ground cumin
- 5g ground coriander
- 5g ground cinnamon
- Salt and pepper to taste

Preparation Instructions:
1. Preheat the Ninja Air Fryer to 375°F using the Bake mode.
2. In a baking dish, combine the chickpeas, sliced carrots, chopped onions, canned diced tomatoes, vegetable broth, ground cumin, ground coriander, ground cinnamon, salt, and pepper.
3. Mix everything together.
4. Cover the baking dish with foil.
5. Place the dish in the air fryer basket.
6. Bake for about 30 minutes or until the carrots are tender and the tagine is hot and fragrant.
7. Remove from the air fryer and let it cool slightly before serving.

Chickpea and Broccoli Stir-Fry

Prep Time: 15 minutes / Cook Time: 10 minutes / Servings: 4

Ingredients:
- 200g chickpeas, cooked
- 300g broccoli florets
- 100g diced red bell peppers
- 100g sliced green onions
- 30ml soy sauce
- 15ml olive oil
- 5g minced garlic
- 5g ground ginger
- Salt and pepper to taste

Preparation Instructions:
1. Preheat the Ninja Air Fryer to 375°F using the Stir-Fry mode.
2. In a bowl, combine the cooked chickpeas, broccoli florets, diced red bell peppers, and sliced green onions.
3. In a separate bowl, whisk together the soy sauce, olive oil, minced garlic, ground ginger, salt, and pepper.
4. Pour the sauce over the chickpea and broccoli mixture and toss to coat.
5. Place the mixture in the air fryer basket.
6. Stir-fry for about 10 minutes or until the vegetables are tender and the chickpeas are heated through.
7. Remove from the air fryer and serve your Chickpea and Broccoli Stir-Fry.

Mushroom and Spinach Shepherd's Pie

Prep Time: 20 minutes / Cook Time: 40 minutes / Servings: 4

Ingredients:
- 400g mushrooms, sliced
- 200g fresh spinach
- 200g onions, chopped
- 200g cooked lentils
- 300g mashed potatoes
- 30ml olive oil
- 5g dried thyme
- Salt and pepper to taste

Preparation Instructions:
1. Preheat the Ninja Air Fryer to 375°F using the Bake mode.
2. In a skillet, heat the olive oil and sauté the chopped onions until they're translucent.
3. Add the sliced mushrooms and cook until they release their moisture and start to brown.
4. Stir in the fresh spinach and cook until it wilts.
5. Add the cooked lentils and dried thyme. Season with salt and pepper.
6. Transfer the mushroom and spinach mixture to a baking dish.
7. Spread the mashed potatoes on top, creating a smooth layer.
8. Place the baking dish in the air fryer basket.
9. Bake for about 40 minutes or until the top is golden brown and the filling is bubbling.
10. Remove from the air fryer and let it cool slightly before serving.

Quinoa and Pomegranate Salad

Prep Time: 15 minutes / Cook Time: 15 minutes / Servings: 4

Ingredients:
- 200g quinoa
- 400ml water
- 100g pomegranate seeds

- 50g chopped fresh parsley
- 30ml olive oil
- 15ml lemon juice
- Salt and pepper to taste

Preparation Instructions:

1. Preheat the Ninja Air Fryer to 375°F using the Air Fry mode.
2. In a saucepan, combine quinoa and water. Bring it to a boil, then reduce the heat, cover, and simmer for 15 minutes or until the quinoa is cooked.
3. Fluff the cooked quinoa with a fork and let it cool.
4. In a mixing bowl, combine the cooked quinoa, pomegranate seeds, chopped fresh parsley, olive oil, lemon juice, salt, and pepper.
5. Toss the Ingredients to combine.
6. Serve your Quinoa and Pomegranate Salad chilled.

Quinoa and Roasted Veggie Bowl

Prep Time: 15 minutes / Cook Time: 20 minutes / Servings: 4

Ingredients:

- 200g quinoa
- 400ml vegetable broth
- 300g mixed roasted vegetables (e. g. , bell peppers, zucchini, and cherry tomatoes)
- 100g baby spinach
- 30ml balsamic vinegar
- 15ml olive oil
- 5g dried oregano
- Salt and pepper to taste

Preparation Instructions:

1. Preheat the Ninja Air Fryer to 375°F using the Bake mode.
2. In a saucepan, combine quinoa and vegetable broth. Bring it to a boil, then reduce the heat, cover, and simmer for 15 minutes or until the quinoa is cooked.
3. In a mixing bowl, toss the mixed roasted vegetables with olive oil, dried oregano, salt, and pepper.
4. Roast the vegetables in the air fryer for about 10 minutes or until they are tender and slightly caramelised.
5. In a serving bowl, combine the cooked quinoa, roasted vegetables, and baby spinach.
6. Drizzle balsamic vinegar over the bowl and toss to combine.
7. Serve your Quinoa and Roasted Veggie Bowl hot or at room temperature.

Bean and Swiss Chard Casserole

Prep Time: 15 minutes / Cook Time: 40 minutes / Servings: 4

Ingredients:

- 200g canned white beans
- 200g Swiss chard, chopped
- 200g onions, chopped
- 100g bell peppers, chopped
- 100g canned diced tomatoes
- 30ml olive oil
- 5g dried basil
- Salt and pepper to taste

Preparation Instructions:

1. Preheat the Ninja Air Fryer to 375°F using the Bake mode.
2. In a skillet, heat the olive oil and sauté the chopped onions until they're translucent.
3. Add the bell peppers and Swiss chard, and cook until they're tender.
4. Stir in the canned white beans, canned diced tomatoes, dried basil, salt, and pepper.
5. Transfer the mixture to a baking dish.
6. Cover the baking dish with foil.
7. Place the dish in the air fryer basket.
8. Bake for about 40 minutes or until the casserole is hot and bubbling.
9. Remove from the air fryer and let it cool slightly before serving.

Red Bean and Corn Chilli

Prep Time: 20 minutes / Cook Time: 30 minutes / Servings: 4

Ingredients:

- 200g red kidney beans
- 200g corn kernels
- 200g diced tomatoes
- 200g onions, chopped
- 5g Chilli powder
- 5g ground cumin
- 5g paprika
- Salt and pepper to taste

Preparation Instructions:

1. Preheat the Ninja Air Fryer to 375°F using the Bake mode.
2. In a baking dish, combine the red kidney beans, corn kernels, diced tomatoes, and chopped onions.
3. Add Chilli powder, ground cumin, paprika, salt,

and pepper.
4. Mix everything together.
5. Cover the baking dish with foil.
6. Place the dish in the air fryer basket.
7. Bake for about 30 minutes or until the Chilli is hot and flavorful.
8. Remove from the air fryer and let it cool slightly before serving.

Red Lentil and Coconut Dahl

Prep Time: 15 minutes / Cook Time: 25 minutes / Servings: 4

Ingredients:
- 200g red lentils
- 400ml coconut milk
- 200g onions, chopped
- 5g ground turmeric
- 5g ground cumin
- 5g ground coriander
- Salt and pepper to taste

Preparation Instructions:
1. Preheat the Ninja Air Fryer to 375°F using the Bake mode.
2. In a baking dish, combine the red lentils, chopped onions, coconut milk, ground turmeric, ground cumin, ground coriander, salt, and pepper.
3. Mix everything together.
4. Cover the baking dish with foil.
5. Place the dish in the air fryer basket.
6. Bake for about 25 minutes or until the lentils are soft and the dahl is hot and aromatic.
7. Remove from the air fryer and let it cool slightly before serving.

Mushroom and Spinach Pasta

Prep Time: 15 minutes / Cook Time: 20 minutes / Servings: 4

Ingredients:
- 300g pasta of your choice
- 200g mushrooms, sliced
- 200g fresh spinach
- 100g onions, chopped
- 2 cloves garlic, minced
- 30ml olive oil
- 30ml heavy cream
- 30g grated Parmesan cheese
- Salt and pepper to taste

Preparation Instructions:
1. Preheat the Ninja Air Fryer to 375°F using the Air Fry mode.
2. Cook the pasta according to the package instructions until al dente. Drain and set aside.
3. In a skillet, heat the olive oil over medium heat.
4. Add the chopped onions and minced garlic. Sauté until the onions become translucent.
5. Add the sliced mushrooms and cook until they release their moisture and start to brown.
6. Stir in the fresh spinach and cook until it wilts.
7. Pour in the heavy cream and stir until it's well combined with the mushroom and spinach mixture.
8. Add the cooked pasta to the skillet and toss to coat everything evenly.
9. Season with salt and pepper to taste.
10. Transfer the pasta mixture to a baking dish.
11. Sprinkle grated Parmesan cheese on top.
12. Place the baking dish in the air fryer basket.
13. Air fry for about 10 minutes or until the pasta is heated through, and the cheese is melted and slightly browned.
14. Remove from the air fryer and let it cool slightly before serving.

Autumn Oat Bake

Prep Time: 10 minutes / Cook time: 20 minutes / Serves 7

Ingredients
- 400g old-fashioned oats
- 2 tsp coconut oil, melted
- 2 small eggs, beaten
- 1 ½ cups full-fat coconut milk
- 2 small apples, cored, peeled, and sliced
- 1 tsp baking powder
- 1/2 cup honey
- A pinch of ground cinnamon
- 1 tsp vanilla bean paste
- A pinch of grated nutmeg

Preparation Instructions
1. Brush the inside of two oven-safe baking tins with coconut oil. Thoroughly combine all the Ingredients and spoon the mixture into the baking tins.
2. Select zone 1 and pair it with "BAKE" at 190°C for 20 minutes. Select "MATCH" to duplicate settings across both zones. Press the "START/ STOP" button.
3. When zone 1 time reaches 10 minutes, turn the baking tins and reinsert the drawers to continue cooking.
4. Bon appétit!

Rustic Qinoa Porridge

Prep Time: 10 minutes / Cook time: 15 minutes / Serves 4

Ingredients

- 2 tsp coconut oil, melted
- 350g quinoa, soaked overnight and rinsed
- 1 tbsp cocoa powder
- 100g dried apricots, pitted and chopped
- 2 large bananas, peeled and mashed
- 1 litre milk
- 1 vanilla bean, split
- 1 cinnamon stick

Preparation Instructions

1. Brush the inside of two oven-safe baking tins with coconut oil.
2. Mix the quinoa with the other Ingredients and spoon the mixture into the baking tins. Add the baking tins to the drawers.
3. Select zone 1 and pair it with "BAKE" at 180°C for 15 minutes. Select "MATCH" to duplicate settings across both zones. Press the "START/ STOP" button.
4. When zone 1 time reaches 7 minutes, rotate both baking tins and reinsert the drawers to continue cooking.
5. Bon appétit!

Black Bean Tacos with Avocado Crema

Prep Time: 10 minutes / Cook Time: 6 minutes / Servings: 2

Ingredients:

- For the tacos:
- 1 can (425g) black beans, drained and rinsed
- 1 teaspoon olive oil
- 1 small onion, finely chopped
- 2 cloves garlic, minced
- 1 teaspoon ground cumin
- 1 teaspoon chili powder
- Salt and pepper to taste
- Tortillas (corn or flour)
- For the avocado crema:
- 1 ripe avocado
- 20ml plain Greek yogurt
- 1 tablespoon lime juice
- Salt to taste

Preparation Instructions:

1. Preheat your Ninja Dual Zone Air Fryer to 200°C.
2. In a skillet over medium heat, warm the olive oil. Add the chopped onion, minced garlic, and sauté until the onion becomes translucent.
3. Add the skillet's black beans, cumin, chili powder, salt, and pepper. Stir well to combine, and cook for 3-4 minutes until the beans are heated.
4. Meanwhile, prepare the avocado crema by blending the avocado, Greek yogurt, lime juice, and salt in a food processor or blender until smooth and creamy. Set this aside.
5. Warm your tortillas in the air fryer for a few seconds until they are pliable.
6. To assemble the tacos, spoon the black bean mixture onto the tortillas and top using your selected toppings. Drizzle the avocado crema over the tacos.
7. Serve immediately and enjoy the flavorful black bean tacos with avocado crema.

Mexican Rice and Beans

Prep Time: 5 minutes / Cook Time: 18 minutes / Servings: 2

Ingredients:

- 185g long-grain rice
- 1 tablespoon olive oil
- 80g Diced onion
- 75g diced bell pepper
- 2 cloves garlic, minced
- 1 can (425g) of black beans, drained and rinsed
- 1 can (411g) of diced tomatoes
- 1 teaspoon chili powder
- 1/2 teaspoon ground cumin
- Salt and pepper to taste
- Fresh cilantro for garnish

Preparation Instructions:

1. Preheat your Ninja Dual Zone Air Fryer to 182°C.
2. In a skillet over medium heat, heat the olive oil. Add the diced onion, bell pepper, and minced garlic. Sauté until the vegetables become tender.
3. Add the rice to the skillet and cook, stirring frequently, for 2-3 minutes until the rice grains are coated with oil and lightly toasted.
4. Transfer the rice mixture to the air fryer drawer. Add the black beans, diced tomatoes, chili powder, cumin, salt, and pepper. Stir well to combine.
5. Set Zone 1 to "AIR FRY" and put the rice mixture in.
6. Cook the rice and beans in the air fryer for 15-18 minutes, stirring halfway through, until the rice is cooked and fluffy.
7. Once cooked, garnish with fresh cilantro, if desired, and serve hot.

Chapter 3 Family Favourites (British Classics)

Arbroath Smokies

Prep Time: 10 minutes / Cook Time: 20 minutes / Servings: 4

Ingredients:
- 4 Arbroath smokies (smoked haddock)
- 200g potatoes, peeled and sliced
- 100g onions, chopped
- 200ml whole milk
- 30g butter
- Salt and pepper to taste

Preparation Instructions:
1. Preheat the Ninja Air Fryer to 375°F using the Bake mode.
2. In a saucepan, combine the potatoes, chopped onions, and whole milk.
3. Cook over low heat until the potatoes are tender.
4. Remove the saucepan from the heat and strain the potatoes and onions, reserving the milk.
5. In a separate saucepan, melt the butter and gently poach the Arbroath smokies until they're heated through.
6. Place the poached smokies in a baking dish.
7. Mash the cooked potatoes and onions, adding some of the reserved milk to achieve a creamy consistency.
8. Season with salt and pepper.
9. Spread the mashed potato mixture over the smokies in the baking dish.
10. Place the baking dish in the air fryer basket.
11. Bake for about 20 minutes or until the top is golden brown and the dish is hot and bubbling.
12. Remove from the air fryer and let it cool slightly before serving.

Creamed Spinach

Prep Time: 10 minutes / Cook Time: 15 minutes / Servings: 4

Ingredients:
- 200g fresh spinach
- 100ml heavy cream
- 50g grated Parmesan cheese
- 5g minced garlic
- 5g nutmeg
- Salt and pepper to taste

Preparation Instructions:
1. Preheat the Ninja Air Fryer to 375°F using the Bake mode.
2. In a skillet, heat the heavy cream and minced garlic over medium heat.
3. Add the fresh spinach and cook until it wilts.
4. Stir in the grated Parmesan cheese and nutmeg, and season with salt and pepper.
5. Transfer the creamed spinach to a baking dish.
6. Place the baking dish in the air fryer basket.
7. Bake for about 15 minutes or until the creamed spinach is hot and bubbling.
8. Remove from the air fryer and let it cool slightly before serving.

Parsnip Mash

Prep Time: 15 minutes / Cook Time: 20 minutes / Servings: 4

Ingredients:
- 400g parsnips, peeled and sliced
- 200g potatoes, peeled and sliced
- 100ml milk
- 30g butter
- Salt and pepper to taste

Preparation Instructions:
1. Preheat the Ninja Air Fryer to 375°F using the Bake mode.
2. In a saucepan, combine the parsnips and potatoes.
3. Cover with water and bring to a boil. Cook until they are tender.
4. Drain the parsnips and potatoes and return them to the saucepan.
5. Add the milk and butter to the saucepan.
6. Mash the parsnips and potatoes until smooth and creamy. Season with salt and pepper.
7. Transfer the parsnip mash to a serving dish.
8. Place the serving dish in the air fryer basket.
9. Bake for about 20 minutes or until the mash is hot and slightly browned on top.
10. Remove from the air fryer and let it cool slightly before serving.

Piccalilli

Prep Time: 20 minutes / Cook Time: 10 minutes / Servings: 4

Ingredients:
- 200g cauliflower florets
- 200g green beans, trimmed and chopped
- 100g onions, finely chopped

- 100g bell peppers, diced
- 200ml white vinegar
- 100g granulated sugar
- 5g ground mustard
- 5g ground turmeric
- 5g cornstarch
- Salt and pepper to taste

Preparation Instructions:

1. Preheat the Ninja Air Fryer to 375°F using the Bake mode.
2. In a saucepan, combine the cauliflower florets, chopped green beans, finely chopped onions, and diced bell peppers.
3. In a separate saucepan, mix white vinegar, granulated sugar, ground mustard, ground turmeric, cornstarch, salt, and pepper. Heat until the mixture thickens.
4. Pour the vinegar mixture over the vegetables and stir to combine.
5. Transfer the mixture to a baking dish.
6. Place the baking dish in the air fryer basket.
7. Bake for about 10 minutes or until the Piccalilli is hot and slightly caramelised.
8. Remove from the air fryer and let it cool slightly before serving.

Tattie Scones

Prep Time: 15 minutes / Cook Time: 15 minutes / Servings: 4

Ingredients:

- 300g potatoes, peeled and diced
- 50g flour
- 15g butter
- Salt to taste

Preparation Instructions:

1. Preheat the Ninja Air Fryer to 375°F using the Bake mode.
2. Boil the diced potatoes until they are soft and can be mashed.
3. Drain and mash the potatoes, then mix in the flour, butter, and salt.
4. Knead the mixture into a dough.
5. Roll out the dough on a floured surface to about 1/4-inch thickness.
6. Cut the dough into rounds or triangles.
7. Place the tattie scones in a baking dish.
8. Place the baking dish in the air fryer basket.
9. Bake for about 15 minutes or until the tattie scones are slightly golden.
10. Remove from the air fryer and let them cool slightly before serving.

Hot Cross Buns

Prep Time: 20 minutes / Cook Time: 20 minutes / Servings: 12 buns

Ingredients:

- For the Buns:
- 500g all-purpose flour
- 75g granulated sugar
- 7g active dry yeast
- 5g salt
- 200ml warm milk
- 1 egg
- 60g unsalted butter, softened
- 150g currants or raisins
- 5g ground cinnamon
- 5g ground nutmeg
- 5g ground allspice
- 5g ground cloves
- Zest of 1 orange
- For the Crosses:
- 50g all-purpose flour
- 50ml water
- For the Glaze:
- 50g apricot jam or marmalade

Preparation Instructions:

1. In a mixing bowl, combine the warm milk, sugar, and yeast. Let it sit for about 5-10 minutes until frothy.
2. In a large bowl, mix the flour, salt, and spices. Add the yeast mixture, softened butter, and egg. Stir until a dough forms.
3. Knead the dough on a floured surface for about 10 minutes, until it's smooth and elastic. Add the currants (or raisins) and orange zest and knead until they are evenly distributed.
4. Place the dough in a greased bowl, cover with a clean kitchen towel, and let it rise for about 1-2 hours or until it has doubled in size.
5. Preheat the Ninja Air Fryer to 375°F using the Bake mode.
6. Punch down the dough and divide it into 12 equal portions. Shape each portion into a ball and place them on a greased baking sheet, leaving some space between each.
7. In a small bowl, mix the flour and water for the crosses until you have a thick paste. Pipe a cross onto the top of each bun using the paste.
8. Bake the buns in the air fryer for about 15-20 minutes or until they're golden brown and sound hollow when tapped on the bottom.
9. While the buns are still warm, heat the apricot jam or marmalade in a microwave and brush it over the

buns to glaze them.

10. Allow the buns to cool on a wire rack before serving.

Norfolk Plough Pudding

Prep Time: 15 minutes / Cook Time: 45 minutes / Servings: 4

Ingredients:
- 200g flour
- 100g suet
- 200g onions, chopped
- 200g carrots, sliced
- 200g potatoes, peeled and sliced
- 200g parsnips, sliced
- Salt and pepper to taste

Preparation Instructions:
1. Preheat the Ninja Air Fryer to 375°F using the Bake mode.
2. In a bowl, mix the flour and suet with a pinch of salt and enough water to form a soft dough.
3. Roll out the dough on a floured surface to fit the bottom of a greased pudding basin.
4. Layer the chopped onions, sliced carrots, potatoes, and parsnips in the pudding basin.
5. Season with salt and pepper.
6. Place the rolled-out suet pastry on top to seal the pudding.
7. Cover the pudding basin with foil and tie it with kitchen string.
8. Place the basin in the air fryer basket.
9. Bake for about 45 minutes or until the pudding is hot and the vegetables are tender.
10. Remove from the air fryer, remove the foil, and let it cool slightly before serving.

Clapshot

Prep Time: 15 minutes / Cook Time: 20 minutes / Servings: 4

Ingredients:
- 500g potatoes, peeled and diced
- 200g turnips, peeled and diced
- 30g butter
- 60ml milk
- Salt and pepper to taste

Preparation Instructions:
1. Preheat the Ninja Air Fryer to 375°F using the Bake mode.
2. Boil the diced potatoes and turnips until they are tender.
3. Drain and mash the potatoes and turnips together.

4. Add the butter and milk and continue to mash until the mixture is smooth and creamy.
5. Season with salt and pepper to taste.
6. Transfer the Clapshot to a serving dish.
7. Place the dish in the air fryer basket.
8. Bake for about 20 minutes to heat the Clapshot through.
9. Remove from the air fryer and let it cool slightly before serving.

Chicken Korma

Prep Time: 20 minutes / Cook Time: 30 minutes / Servings: 4

Ingredients:
- 500g boneless chicken, diced
- 200g onions, chopped
- 100g tomatoes, chopped
- 100g plain yoghurt
- 30g almonds, ground
- 30g coconut milk
- 10g ginger-garlic paste
- 5g garam masala
- 5g turmeric
- 5g cumin
- 5g coriander
- 5g Chilli powder
- Salt and pepper to taste

Preparation Instructions:
1. Preheat the Ninja Air Fryer to 375°F using the Bake mode.
2. In a skillet, heat some oil and sauté the chopped onions until they're translucent.
3. Add the ginger-garlic paste and cook for a minute.
4. Stir in the diced chicken and cook until it's browned.
5. Add the chopped tomatoes and cook until they soften.
6. Mix in the ground almonds, yoghurt, coconut milk, and spices.
7. Season with salt and pepper.
8. Cover the skillet and bake in the air fryer for about 30 minutes, stirring occasionally, until the chicken is cooked through.
9. Remove from the air fryer and let it cool slightly before serving.

Cornish Splits

Prep Time: 15 minutes / Cook Time: 15 minutes / Servings: 4

- Mode: Bake
- 300g all-purpose flour

- 150ml warm milk
- 30g granulated sugar
- 30g unsalted butter, melted
- 7g active dry yeast
- 5g salt
- Jam and clotted cream for filling

Preparation Instructions:

1. Preheat the Ninja Air Fryer to 375°F using the Bake mode.
2. In a mixing bowl, combine the warm milk, sugar, and yeast. Let it sit for about 5-10 minutes until frothy.
3. Stir in the melted butter and salt.
4. Add the flour and knead until a soft dough forms.
5. Cover the bowl with a clean kitchen towel and let the dough rise for about 1 hour or until it has doubled in size.
6. Punch down the dough and divide it into 4 portions.
7. Shape each portion into a round bun and place them on a greased baking sheet.
8. Bake in the air fryer for about 15 minutes or until the buns are golden brown and sound hollow when tapped on the bottom.
9. Allow the buns to cool, then split them open, fill with jam and clotted cream, and enjoy.

Frumenty

Prep Time: 15 minutes / Cook Time: 30 minutes / Servings: 4

Ingredients:

- 200g wheat grains
- 500ml milk
- 50g honey
- 30g raisins
- 5g ground cinnamon
- 5g ground nutmeg
- 5g ground cloves
- 5g ground allspice

Preparation Instructions:

1. Preheat the Ninja Air Fryer to 375°F using the Bake mode.
2. In a saucepan, combine the wheat grains and milk.
3. Bring the mixture to a boil, then reduce the heat and simmer for about 20 minutes until the grains are soft.
4. Stir in the honey, raisins, and spices.
5. Simmer for another 10 minutes until the mixture thickens.
6. Pour the Frumenty into serving bowls.
7. Place the bowls in the air fryer basket.
8. Bake for about 10 minutes to heat the Frumenty

through.
9. Remove from the air fryer and let it cool slightly before serving.

Rumbledethumps

Prep Time: 20 minutes / Cook Time: 30 minutes / Servings: 4

Ingredients:

- 500g potatoes, peeled and diced
- 200g cabbage, shredded
- 100g turnips, peeled and diced
- 100g butter
- Salt and pepper to taste
- 100g cheddar cheese, grated (optional)

Preparation Instructions:

1. Preheat the Ninja Air Fryer to 375°F using the Bake mode.
2. Boil the diced potatoes and turnips until they are tender.
3. In a separate pot, boil the shredded cabbage until it's soft.
4. Drain the potatoes, turnips, and cabbage, and mash them together with the butter.
5. Season with salt and pepper to taste.
6. Optionally, mix in the grated cheddar cheese for added flavor.
7. Transfer the mixture to a greased baking dish.
8. Bake in the air fryer for about 30 minutes or until the top is golden and the Rumbledethumps are heated through.
9. Remove from the air fryer and let it cool slightly before serving.

Welsh Rarebit Soufflé

Prep Time: 20 minutes / Cook Time: 20 minutes / Servings: 4

Ingredients:

- 200g cheddar cheese, grated
- 4 slices of bread
- 200ml milk
- 50g butter
- 30g all-purpose flour
- 4 eggs, separated
- 5g mustard
- Salt and pepper to taste
- Paprika for garnish (optional)

Preparation Instructions:

1. Preheat the Ninja Air Fryer to 375°F using the Bake mode.
2. In a saucepan, melt the butter over low heat.

3. Stir in the flour to create a roux and cook for a few minutes.
4. Gradually add the milk, stirring continuously until the mixture thickens.
5. Remove the saucepan from the heat and stir in the grated cheddar cheese, mustard, salt, and pepper.
6. Toast the slices of bread and cut them into small squares.
7. In a separate bowl, beat the egg yolks and fold them into the cheese mixture.
8. In another bowl, beat the egg whites until stiff peaks form.
9. Gently fold the beaten egg whites into the cheese mixture.
10. Place the toasted bread squares at the bottom of a greased baking dish.
11. Pour the cheese and egg mixture over the bread.
12. Sprinkle with paprika for garnish if desired.
13. Bake in the air fryer for about 20 minutes or until the soufflé has risen and is golden brown.
14. Remove from the air fryer and let it cool slightly before serving.

Panackelty

Prep Time: 20 minutes / Cook Time: 55 minutes / Servings: 4

Ingredients:
- 500g potatoes, peeled and sliced
- 300g onions, sliced
- 300g bacon, diced
- 300g corned beef, diced
- Salt and pepper to taste

Preparation Instructions:
1. Preheat the Ninja Air Fryer to 375°F using the Bake mode.
2. In a large ovenproof dish, layer the sliced potatoes, onions, diced bacon, and diced corned beef.
3. Season each layer with salt and pepper.
4. Cover the dish with foil or a lid.
5. Bake in the air fryer for about 55 minutes or until the potatoes are tender and the flavors have melded together.
6. Remove from the air fryer and let it cool slightly before serving.

Beef and Oyster Pie

Prep Time: 20 minutes / Cook Time: 30 minutes / Servings: 4

Ingredients:
- 500g beef stewing steak, cubed
- 200g oysters
- 200g onions, chopped
- 200g mushrooms, sliced
- 30g all-purpose flour
- 30g butter
- 300ml beef broth
- Salt and pepper to taste
- Prepared puff pastry

Preparation Instructions:
1. In a pan, melt the butter and sauté the onions and mushrooms until softened.
2. Add the beef and brown it.
3. Sprinkle the flour over the mixture and stir to combine.
4. Pour in the beef broth, season with salt and pepper, and simmer until the beef is tender.
5. Stir in the oysters and cook for a few minutes.
6. Transfer the mixture to a pie dish and cover with puff pastry.
7. Bake until the pastry is golden brown.

Blackberry Cobbler

Prep Time: 15 minutes / Cook Time: 25 minutes / Servings: 4

Ingredients:
- 400g fresh blackberries
- 100g granulated sugar
- 150g all-purpose flour
- 2 tsp baking powder
- 1/2 tsp salt
- 60g unsalted butter, melted
- 200ml milk
- 1 tsp vanilla extract
- 1/2 tsp ground cinnamon (optional)

Preparation Instructions:
1. Preheat the Ninja Air Fryer to 375°F using the Bake mode.
2. In a mixing bowl, combine the blackberries and 50g of sugar. Toss to coat the berries and set aside.
3. In another bowl, whisk together the flour, baking powder, 50g of sugar, and salt.
4. Add the melted butter, milk, vanilla extract, and ground cinnamon (if using) to the dry ingredients. Mix until well combined.
5. Pour the batter into a greased baking dish.
6. Spread the blackberries evenly over the batter.
7. Air fry for about 20-25 minutes or until the cobbler is golden and the berries are bubbling.
8. Serve warm with a scoop of vanilla ice cream or a dollop of whipped cream.

Plaice Goujons

Prep Time: 15 minutes / Cook Time: 10 minutes / Servings: 4

Ingredients:
- 400g plaice fillets, cut into strips
- 100g breadcrumbs
- 2 eggs, beaten
- 30g all-purpose flour
- 1 tsp paprika
- Salt and pepper to taste
- Lemon wedges, for serving

Preparation Instructions:
1. Preheat the Ninja Air Fryer to 375°F using the Air Fry mode.
2. In separate bowls, place the flour, beaten eggs, and breadcrumbs.
3. Season the breadcrumbs with paprika, salt, and pepper.
4. Dredge the plaice strips in the flour, dip them in the beaten eggs, and coat them with the seasoned breadcrumbs.
5. Place the coated plaice goujons in the air fryer basket.
6. Air fry for about 8-10 minutes, turning once, until the goujons are golden and crispy.
7. Serve with lemon wedges and your favorite dipping sauce.

Beef and Onion Pie

Prep Time: 20 minutes / Cook Time: 30 minutes / Servings: 4

Ingredients:
- 500g beef stewing steak, cubed
- 200g onions, chopped
- 200g potatoes, peeled and diced
- 200ml beef broth
- 30g all-purpose flour
- 30g butter
- Salt and pepper to taste
- Prepared shortcrust pastry
- Preparation Preparation:
1. Preheat the Ninja Air Fryer to 375°F using the Bake mode.
2. In a pan, melt the butter and sauté the onions until softened.
3. Add the beef and brown it.
4. Sprinkle the flour over the mixture and stir to combine.
5. Pour in the beef broth, season with salt and pepper, and simmer until the beef is tender.
6. Stir in the diced potatoes and cook until they are tender.
7. Transfer the mixture to a pie dish and cover with the shortcrust pastry.
8. Bake until the pastry is golden brown.

Cheesy Stuffed Peppers

Prep Time: 5 minutes / Cook time: 20 minutes / Serves 6

Ingredients
- 6 medium peppers, deveined
- 400g cooked millet, drained
- 200g cooked or canned red kidney beans, drained
- 1 small tomato, chopped
- Sea salt and ground black pepper, to taste
- 100g Swiss cheese, grated

Preparation Instructions
1. Insert crisper plates in both drawers. Spray the crisper plates with nonstick cooking oil. Place the peppers in both drawers.
2. Select zone 1 and pair it with "ROAST" at 180°C for 10 minutes. Select "MATCH" to duplicate settings across both zones. Press the "START/STOP" button.
3. In a mixing bowl, thoroughly combine the other ingredients. Divide the mixture between bell peppers and arrange the peppers in both drawers of your Ninja Foodi.
4. Select zone 1 and pair it with "BAKE" at 190°C for 10 minutes. Select "MATCH" to duplicate settings across both zones. Press the "START/STOP" button.

Meatloaf with Mashed Potatoes

Prep Time: 10 minutes / Cook time: 20 minutes / Serves 5

Ingredients
- 250g pork mince
- 250 beef mince
- 1 small egg, well-beaten
- 2 tbsp barbecue sauce
- 2 garlic cloves, minced
- 1 small leek, chopped
- Sea salt and ground black pepper
- 50g fresh breadcrumbs
- 1 tbsp olive oil
- 170ml tomato paste
- 1 tbsp English mustard
- 500g baby potatoes, scrubbed
- 1 tbsp butter, room temperature

Preparation Instructions

1. Brush a loaf tin with nonstick cooking oil.
2. In a mixing bowl, thoroughly combine the pork mince, beef mince, egg, barbecue sauce, garlic, leek, salt, pepper, and breadcrumbs. Press the mixture into the prepared loaf tin and brush it with olive oil.
3. Whisk the tomato paste and mustard until well combined; reserve.
4. Add the meatloaf to the zone 1 drawer. Toss baby potatoes with salt and pepper; spray the potatoes with cooking oil and place them in the zone 2 drawer.
5. Select zone 1 and pair it with "BAKE" at 180°C for 20 minutes. Select zone 2 and pair it with "ROAST" at 200°C for about 18 minutes. Select "SYNC" followed by the "START/STOP" button.
6. When zone 1 time reaches 10 minutes, spread the tomato mixture over the top of your meatloaf. Reinsert the drawer to continue cooking. (Cook until the centre of your meatloaf reaches 74°C).
7. Toss baby potatoes to ensure even cooking. Mash baby potatoes with butter and serve immediately.

Carnitas Enchiladas

Prep Time: 10 minutes / Cook time: 1 hour 10 minutes / Serves 4

Ingredients

- 800g pork shoulder, cut into 4 pieces
- 1 tsp olive oil
- Sea salt and ground black pepper, to taste
- 8 small corn tortillas
- Enchilada Sauce:
- 1 tbsp olive oil
- 1 tsp ground cumin
- 1 tsp garlic powder
- 3 tbsp tomato paste
- 200ml chicken broth
- 1 tbsp fresh lime juice
- 1 jalapeño pepper, deveined

Preparation Instructions

1. Insert crisper plates in zone 1 and 2 drawers. Spray the crisper plates with nonstick cooking oil.
2. Toss pork shoulder with 1 teaspoon of olive oil, salt, and black pepper. Divide the pork shoulder between both drawers.
3. Select zone 1 and pair it with "ROAST" at 175°C

for 55 minutes. Select "MATCH" to duplicate settings across both zones. Press the "START/STOP" button.
4. At the halfway point, gently flip the meat, and reinsert the drawers to resume cooking.
5. Meanwhile, mix all the sauce Ingredients until well combined.
6. Shred the pork with two forks and divide it between tortillas; top with cheese and roll tightly to assemble your enchiladas.
7. Divide enchiladas between two lightly greased baking tins; spoon the sauce over them and add them to both drawers (without crisper plates).
8. Select zone 1 and pair it with "BAKE" at 190°C for 15 minutes, until the edges of the tortillas are slightly browned. Select "MATCH" to duplicate settings across both zones. Press the "START/STOP" button.
9. Bon appétit!

Tuna Jacket Potatoes

Prep Time: 10 minutes / Cook time: 35 minutes / Serves 4

Ingredients

- 4 (220g each) russet potatoes
- 2 tsp English mustard
- 1 (185g) can tuna in oil, drained
- 2 spring onions, sliced
- 4 sun-dried tomatoes in oil, chopped
- 6 tbsp sour cream
- 1 small chilli, minced
- Sea salt and ground black pepper, to taste

Preparation Instructions

1. Pierce your potatoes with a fork a few times. Place the potatoes in both drawers.
2. Select zone 1 and pair it with "BAKE" at 200°C for 35 minutes. Select "MATCH" to duplicate settings across both zones. Press the "START/STOP" button.
3. Meanwhile, mix the remaining Ingredients for the filling.
4. When zone 1 time reaches 20 minutes, split the potatoes down the middle. Now, divide the filling between your potatoes; reinsert the drawers to continue cooking.
5. Taste, adjust the seasoning and enjoy!

Chicken Saag

Prep Time: 20 minutes / Cook Time: 30 minutes / Servings: 4

Ingredients:
- 500g chicken, cut into pieces
- 500g spinach, washed and chopped
- 1 large onion, chopped
- 2 cloves garlic, minced
- 1-inch piece of ginger, minced
- 120ml tomato sauce
- 2 tablespoons vegetable oil
- 1 teaspoon cumin seeds
- 1/2 teaspoon turmeric
- 1/2 teaspoon garam masala
- Salt to taste

Preparation Instructions:
1. Preheat the Ninja Air Fryer to 375°F using the Air Fry mode.
2. Heat vegetable oil in a pan. Add cumin seeds and sauté until they sizzle.
3. Add the chopped onions and sauté until they turn translucent.
4. Stir in the minced garlic and ginger and cook for a couple of minutes.
5. Add the chicken pieces and cook until they are no longer pink.
6. Add the chopped spinach, turmeric, and garam masala. Cook until the spinach wilts.
7. Stir in the tomato sauce and simmer for a few minutes.
8. Transfer the mixture to the air fryer basket and air fry for about 15-20 minutes until the chicken is fully cooked and the flavors meld.

Chicken Madras

Prep Time: 15 minutes / Cook Time: 25 minutes / Servings: 4

Ingredients:
- 500g chicken, cut into pieces
- 2 onions, chopped
- 2 tomatoes, chopped
- 2 cloves garlic, minced
- 1-inch piece of ginger, minced
- 2 tablespoons vegetable oil
- 2 tablespoons Madras curry powder
- 1/2 teaspoon turmeric
- 1/2 teaspoon red Chilli powder
- 1/2 teaspoon cumin seeds
- 120ml coconut milk
- Salt to taste

Preparation Instructions:
1. Preheat the Ninja Air Fryer to 375°F using the Air Fry mode.
2. Heat vegetable oil in a pan. Add cumin seeds and sauté until they sizzle.
3. Add the chopped onions and sauté until they turn translucent.
4. Stir in the minced garlic and ginger and cook for a couple of minutes.
5. Add the chicken pieces and cook until they are no longer pink.
6. Add the chopped tomatoes, Madras curry powder, turmeric, and red Chilli powder. Cook until the tomatoes are soft.
7. Stir in the coconut milk and simmer for a few minutes.
8. Transfer the mixture to the air fryer basket and air fry for about 15-20 minutes until the chicken is fully cooked and the flavors meld.

Quail with Wild Mushrooms

Prep Time: 15 minutes / Cook Time: 30 minutes / Servings: 4

Ingredients:
- 4 quail, cleaned
- 200g wild mushrooms, cleaned and sliced
- 1 onion, finely chopped
- 2 cloves garlic, minced
- 2 tablespoons fresh thyme, chopped
- Salt and pepper to taste
- 2 tablespoons butter

Preparation Instructions:
1. Preheat the Ninja Air Fryer to 375°F using the Roast mode.
2. In a pan, melt the butter and sauté the chopped onion and minced garlic until they are soft.
3. Add the wild mushrooms and fresh thyme to the pan and cook until the mushrooms are tender.
4. Season the quail with salt and pepper.
5. Stuff the quail with the cooked mushroom mixture.
6. Place the stuffed quail in the air fryer basket.
7. Roast the quail for about 30 minutes, or until they are cooked through and the skin is crispy.

8. Remove the quail from the air fryer and let them rest for a few minutes before serving.

Grouse with Game Chips

Prep Time: 20 minutes / Cook Time: 30 minutes / Servings: 4

Ingredients:
- 4 grouse, cleaned
- 4 large potatoes (about 800g), peeled and cut into thick chips
- 30ml vegetable oil
- 2 tablespoons fresh rosemary, chopped
- Salt and pepper to taste
- 30g butter

Preparation Instructions:
1. Preheat the Ninja Air Fryer to 375°F using the Roast mode.
2. In a mixing bowl, toss the potato chips with 30ml of vegetable oil, chopped rosemary, salt, and pepper.
3. Place the seasoned potato chips in the air fryer basket.
4. Roast the potato chips for about 15-20 minutes until they are golden and crispy. Shake the basket occasionally for even cooking.
5. While the chips are roasting, season the grouse with salt and pepper.
6. In a separate pan, melt 30g of butter and sear the grouse until they are browned on all sides.
7. Place the seared grouse in the air fryer basket.
8. Roast the grouse for about 10-15 minutes until they are cooked to your desired doneness.
9. Serve the Grouse with Game Chips with the crispy potato chips on the side.

Chicken Pasanda

Prep Time: 15 minutes / Cook Time: 20 minutes / Servings: 4

Ingredients:
- 500g boneless chicken, cut into pieces
- 2 onions, finely chopped
- 2 cloves garlic, minced
- 1-inch piece of ginger, minced
- 120ml plain yoghurt
- 20g ground almonds
- 2 tablespoons vegetable oil
- 1 teaspoon ground coriander
- 2g ground cumin
- 2g ground turmeric
- 2g garam masala
- Salt to taste

Preparation Instructions:
1. Preheat the Ninja Air Fryer to 375°F using the Air Fry mode.
2. In a pan, heat 2 tablespoons of vegetable oil and sauté the chopped onions until they are soft and golden.
3. Stir in the minced garlic and ginger and cook for a few minutes.
4. Add the chicken pieces and cook until they are no longer pink.
5. In a bowl, mix the plain yoghurt, ground almonds, 1 teaspoon of ground coriander, 2g of ground cumin, 2g of ground turmeric, 2g of garam masala, and salt.
6. Stir the yoghurt and almond mixture into the pan with the chicken. Simmer for a few minutes.
7. Transfer the chicken and sauce to the air fryer basket.
8. Air fry the Chicken Pasanda for about 15-20 minutes until the chicken is fully cooked and the sauce thickens.

Chicken Dhansak

Prep Time: 15 minutes / Cook Time: 30 minutes / Servings: 4

Ingredients:
- 500g boneless chicken, cut into pieces
- 200g red lentils
- 1 onion, chopped
- 2 cloves garlic, minced
- 1-inch piece of ginger, minced
- 1 teaspoon ground turmeric
- 1 teaspoon ground cumin
- 1 teaspoon ground coriander
- 1 teaspoon garam masala
- Salt and pepper to taste
- 1 tablespoon vegetable oil
- 500ml chicken broth

Preparation Instructions:
1. Preheat the Ninja Air Fryer to 375°F using the Air Fry mode.
2. In a pan, heat 1 tablespoon of vegetable oil and sauté the chopped onion until it's soft and translucent.
3. Add the minced garlic and ginger, and cook for a few minutes.
4. Stir in the ground turmeric, ground cumin, ground coriander, and garam masala.
5. Add the chicken pieces and brown them.
6. Rinse the red lentils and add them to the pan.
7. Pour in 500ml of chicken broth and bring to a simmer.

8. Season with salt and pepper to taste.
9. Transfer the mixture to the air fryer basket.
10. Air fry for about 25-30 minutes, until the chicken is fully cooked and the lentils are tender.
11. Serve the Chicken Dhansak with rice or naan bread.

Pigeon and Pancetta Salad

Prep Time: 10 minutes / Cook Time: 10 minutes / Servings: 2

Ingredients:
- 4 pigeon breasts
- 100g pancetta
- 100g mixed salad greens
- 1 red onion, thinly sliced
- 2 tablespoons balsamic vinegar
- 2 tablespoons olive oil
- Salt and pepper to taste

Preparation Instructions:
1. Preheat the Ninja Air Fryer to 375°F using the Roast mode.
2. In a bowl, toss the pigeon breasts with olive oil, salt, and pepper.
3. Place the pigeon breasts in the air fryer basket.
4. Roast for about 8-10 minutes, or until they are cooked to your desired doneness.
5. In a separate pan, crisp the pancetta.
6. In a bowl, whisk together the balsamic vinegar and olive oil to make the dressing.
7. In a large bowl, toss the mixed salad greens and sliced red onion with the dressing.
8. Divide the salad onto two plates, top with the roasted pigeon breasts and crispy pancetta.

Chicken Methi

Prep Time: 15 minutes / Cook Time: 30 minutes / Servings: 4

Ingredients:
- 500g boneless chicken, cut into pieces
- 60g (2 cups) fresh fenugreek leaves (methi), chopped
- 1 onion, chopped
- 2 cloves garlic, minced
- 1-inch piece of ginger, minced
- 2 tomatoes, chopped
- 1 teaspoon ground turmeric
- 1 teaspoon ground cumin
- 1 teaspoon ground coriander
- 1/2 teaspoon red Chilli powder (adjust to taste)
- Salt to taste
- 2 tablespoons vegetable oil

Preparation Instructions:
1. Preheat the Ninja Air Fryer to 375°F using the Air Fry mode.
2. In a pan, heat 2 tablespoons of vegetable oil and sauté the chopped onion until it's soft and translucent.
3. Add the minced garlic and ginger, and cook for a few minutes.
4. Stir in the ground turmeric, ground cumin, ground coriander, and red Chilli powder.
5. Add the chicken pieces and brown them.
6. Add the chopped tomatoes and fenugreek leaves.
7. Season with salt to taste.
8. Transfer the mixture to the air fryer basket.
9. Air fry for about 25-30 minutes, until the chicken is fully cooked and the fenugreek leaves are tender.
10. Serve the Chicken Methi with rice or naan bread.

Chicken Pathia

Prep Time: 15 minutes / Cook Time: 30 minutes / Servings: 4

Ingredients:
- 500g boneless chicken, cut into pieces
- 1 onion, chopped
- 2 cloves garlic, minced
- 1-inch piece of ginger, minced
- 2 tomatoes, chopped
- 2 tablespoons tamarind paste
- 1 teaspoon ground turmeric
- 1 teaspoon ground cumin
- 1 teaspoon ground coriander
- 1/2 teaspoon red Chilli powder (adjust to taste)
- Salt to taste
- 2 tablespoons vegetable oil

Preparation Instructions:
1. Preheat the Ninja Air Fryer to 375°F using the Air Fry mode.
2. In a pan, heat 2 tablespoons of vegetable oil and sauté the chopped onion until it's soft and translucent.
3. Add the minced garlic and ginger, and cook for a few minutes.
4. Stir in the ground turmeric, ground cumin, ground coriander, and red Chilli powder.
5. Add the chicken pieces and brown them.
6. Add the chopped tomatoes and tamarind paste.
7. Season with salt to taste.
8. Transfer the mixture to the air fryer basket.
9. Air fry for about 25-30 minutes, until the chicken is fully cooked and the sauce thickens.
10. Serve the Chicken Pathia with rice or naan bread.

Chicken Vindaloo

Prep Time: 15 minutes / Cook Time: 30 minutes / Servings: 4

Ingredients:

- 500g boneless chicken, cut into pieces
- 1 onion, chopped
- 2 cloves garlic, minced
- 1-inch piece of ginger, minced
- 2 tomatoes, chopped
- 2 tablespoons malt vinegar
- 1 teaspoon ground turmeric
- 1 teaspoon ground cumin
- 1 teaspoon ground coriander
- 1/2 teaspoon red Chilli powder (adjust to taste)
- Salt to taste
- 2 tablespoons vegetable oil

Preparation Instructions:

1. Preheat the Ninja Air Fryer to 375°F using the Air Fry mode.
2. In a pan, heat 2 tablespoons of vegetable oil and sauté the chopped onion until it's soft and translucent.
3. Add the minced garlic and ginger, and cook for a few minutes.
4. Stir in the ground turmeric, ground cumin, ground coriander, and red Chilli powder.
5. Add the chicken pieces and brown them.
6. Add the chopped tomatoes and malt vinegar.
7. Season with salt to taste.
8. Transfer the mixture to the air fryer basket.
9. Air fry for about 25-30 minutes, until the chicken is fully cooked and the sauce thickens.
10. Serve the Chicken Vindaloo with rice or naan bread.

Chicken and Leek Gratin

Prep Time: 15 minutes / Cook Time: 30 minutes / Servings: 4

Ingredients:

- 500g boneless chicken, cut into pieces
- 2 leeks, sliced
- 2 cloves garlic, minced
- 240ml heavy cream
- 60g grated cheese
- 30g bread crumbs
- 30g butter
- Salt and pepper to taste

Preparation Instructions:

1. Preheat the Ninja Air Fryer to 375°F using the Bake mode.
2. In a pan, melt the butter and sauté the leeks and minced garlic until they are soft.
3. Add the chicken pieces and cook until they are no longer pink.
4. Season with salt and pepper to taste.
5. In a separate bowl, mix the heavy cream (240ml) and grated cheese (60g).
6. Transfer the chicken and leek mixture to an ovenproof dish.
7. Pour the cream and cheese mixture over the top.
8. Sprinkle the bread crumbs (30g) over the dish.
9. Place the dish in the air fryer basket.
10. Bake for about 25-30 minutes, until the top is golden and the gratin is bubbling.
11. Serve hot and ejoy.

Chicken and Gammon Pie

Prep Time: 15 minutes / Cook Time: 45 minutes / Servings: 4

Ingredients:

- 500g boneless chicken, cut into pieces
- 200g gammon, diced
- 1 onion, chopped
- 2 cloves garlic, minced
- 240ml chicken broth
- 120ml heavy cream
- 30g all-purpose flour
- 1 sheet puff pastry
- 30g vegetable oil
- Salt and pepper to taste

Preparation Instructions:

1. Preheat the Ninja Air Fryer to 375°F using the Bake mode.
2. In a pan, heat the vegetable oil and sauté the chopped onion and minced garlic until they are soft.
3. Add the chicken and gammon and cook until they are browned.
4. Stir in the all-purpose flour (30g) and cook for a few minutes.
5. Pour in the chicken broth (240ml) and heavy cream (120ml).
6. Season with salt and pepper to taste.
7. Transfer the mixture to an ovenproof dish.
8. Cover the dish with the puff pastry sheet, trimming any excess.
9. Make a few slits in the pastry to allow steam to escape.
10. Place the dish in the air fryer basket.
11. Bake for about 40-45 minutes, until the pastry is golden and the filling is hot and bubbling.
12. Serve your Chicken and Gammon Pie with your

favorite sides.

Guinea Fowl and Orange Glaze

Prep Time: 15 minutes / Cook Time: 45 minutes /
Servings: 4

Ingredients:
- 4 guinea fowl breasts
- 2 oranges, juiced and zested
- 2 tablespoons honey
- 2 tablespoons olive oil
- 2 cloves garlic, minced
- Salt and pepper to taste

Preparation Instructions:
1. Preheat the Ninja Air Fryer to 375°F using the Bake mode.
2. In a bowl, mix the orange juice and zest, honey, olive oil, and minced garlic.
3. Season the guinea fowl breasts with salt and pepper.
4. Place the guinea fowl breasts in a shallow dish and pour the orange glaze over them.
5. Let them marinate for about 15 minutes.
6. Transfer the guinea fowl breasts to an ovenproof dish, reserving the marinade.
7. Bake for about 40-45 minutes, occasionally basting with the marinade, until the guinea fowl is cooked through and the glaze is caramelised.
8. Serve hot and enjoy.

Chicken and Leek Cannelloni

Prep Time: 20 minutes / Cook Time: 40 minutes /
Servings: 4

Ingredients:
- 8 cannelloni tubes
- 2 chicken breasts, cooked and shredded
- 2 leeks, sliced
- 200ml heavy cream
- 60g grated cheese
- 2 tablespoons butter
- Salt and pepper to taste

Preparation Instructions:
1. Preheat the Ninja Air Fryer to 375°F using the Bake mode.
2. In a pan, melt the butter and sauté the sliced leeks until they are soft.
3. Add the cooked, shredded chicken and cook for a few minutes.
4. Season with salt and pepper to taste.
5. In a separate bowl, mix the heavy cream and grated cheese.
6. Fill the cannelloni tubes with the chicken and leek

mixture.
7. Place the filled cannelloni tubes in an ovenproof dish.
8. Pour the cream and cheese mixture over the top.
9. Bake for about 35-40 minutes, until the cannelloni is cooked and the top is golden and bubbly.
10. Serve hot and enjoy with family.

Turkey and Mushroom Phyllo Tarts

Prep Time: 20 minutes / Cook Time: 25 minutes /
Servings: 4

Ingredients:
- 8 sheets phyllo pastry
- 480 ml cooked turkey, shredded
- 240 ml mushrooms, sliced
- 1 small onion, finely chopped
- 2 cloves garlic, minced
- 60g grated cheese
- 30ml olive oil
- Salt and pepper to taste

Preparation Instructions:
1. Preheat the Ninja Air Fryer to 374°F using the Bake mode.
2. In a pan, heat the olive oil and sauté the chopped onion and minced garlic until they are soft.
3. Add the sliced mushrooms and cook until they release their moisture and it evaporates.
4. Stir in the shredded turkey and season with salt and pepper.
5. Lay out a sheet of phyllo pastry and brush it lightly with olive oil. Repeat with another sheet and place it on top.
6. Spoon a portion of the turkey and mushroom mixture onto the phyllo sheets.
7. Sprinkle with grated cheese.
8. Carefully fold the phyllo sheets over the filling to create a tart.
9. Repeat for the remaining tarts.
10. Place the tarts in the air fryer basket and bake for about 20-25 minutes, or until the phyllo is golden and crispy.
11. Serve your Turkey and Mushroom Phyllo Tarts hot.

Turkey and Spinach Phyllo Parcels

Prep Time: 20 minutes / Cook Time: 25 minutes /
Servings: 4

Ingredients:
- 8 sheets phyllo pastry
- 480g cooked turkey, shredded
- 480ml fresh spinach

- 60ml red bell pepper, finely chopped
- 240ml onion, finely chopped
- 2 cloves garlic, minced
- 120 g feta cheese, crumbled
- 60 ml olive oil
- Salt and pepper to taste

Preparation Instructions:

1. Preheat the Ninja Air Fryer to 374°F using the Bake mode.
2. In a pan, heat the olive oil and sauté the chopped onion and minced garlic until they are soft.
3. Add the red bell pepper and cook for a few minutes until it's softened.
4. Stir in the shredded turkey and fresh spinach. Cook until the spinach wilts and the mixture is heated through. Season with salt and pepper.
5. Lay out a sheet of phyllo pastry and brush it lightly with olive oil. Repeat with another sheet and place it on top.
6. Spoon a portion of the turkey and spinach mixture onto the phyllo sheets.
7. Sprinkle with crumbled feta cheese.
8. Carefully fold the phyllo sheets over the filling to create a parcel.
9. Repeat for the remaining parcels.
10. Place the parcels in the air fryer basket and bake for about 20-25 minutes, or until the phyllo is golden and crispy.
11. Serve your Turkey and Spinach Phyllo Parcels hot.

Chicken and Thyme Gratin

Prep Time: 15 minutes / Cook Time: 30 minutes / Servings: 4

Ingredients:

- 480g cooked chicken, shredded
- 480g potatoes, thinly sliced
- 240ml leeks, sliced
- 60ml cream
- 60ml chicken broth
- 2 cloves garlic, minced
- 2 tablespoons fresh thyme leaves
- Salt and pepper to taste

Preparation Instructions:

1. Preheat the Ninja Air Fryer to 374°F using the Bake mode.
2. In a bowl, mix the sliced potatoes, leeks, minced garlic, and fresh thyme leaves.
3. In a separate bowl, combine the cream and chicken broth. Season with salt and pepper.
4. In individual baking dishes, layer the shredded chicken, potato and leek mixture.
5. Pour the cream and chicken broth mixture over the top.
6. Place the dishes in the air fryer basket.
7. Bake for about 25-30 minutes, or until the potatoes are tender and the top is golden.
8. Serve your Chicken and Thyme Gratin hot.

Turkey and Sausage Jambalaya

Prep Time: 15 minutes / Cook Time: 30 minutes / Servings: 4

Ingredients:

- 480g cooked turkey, cubed
- 240g smoked sausage, sliced
- 240g bell pepper, diced
- 240g onion, finely chopped
- 240ml celery, diced
- 2 cloves garlic, minced
- 480ml rice
- 960ml chicken broth
- 1 can (400g) diced tomatoes
- 2 tablespoons Cajun seasoning
- Salt and pepper to taste

Preparation Instructions:

1. Preheat the Ninja Air Fryer to 392°F using the Air Fry mode.
2. In a large pan, heat some olive oil and sauté the onion, celery, and bell pepper until they're soft.
3. Add the garlic and cook for another minute.
4. Stir in the rice and cook for a few minutes until it's well-coated.
5. Add the diced tomatoes, chicken broth, Cajun seasoning, salt, and pepper.
6. Stir in the cooked turkey and sliced smoked sausage.
7. Transfer the mixture to the air fryer basket.
8. Air fry for about 20-25 minutes, or until the rice is tender and the jambalaya is heated through.
9. Serve your Turkey and Sausage Jambalaya hot.

Indian Tandoori Chicken Skewers

Prep Time: 10 minutes / Marination time: 2-4 hours / Cook time: 20 minutes / Serves: 4

Ingredients:

- 4 boneless chicken breasts, cut into bite-sized cubes
- 480g plain Greek yoghurt
- 2 tbsp tandoori masala spice blend
- 1 tbsp fresh lemon juice
- 2 cloves garlic, minced
- Salt, to taste

- 1 green bell pepper, cut into bite-sized pieces
- 1 red onion, cut into bite-sized pieces
- Skewers, soaked in water for at least 30 minutes

Preparation Instructions:

1. In a bowl, mix together the Greek yoghurt, tandoori masala spice blend, lemon juice, minced garlic, and salt.
2. Add the chicken cubes to the marinade, making sure they are well coated. Cover the bowl with plastic wrap and refrigerate for at least 2 hours or up to 4 hours.
3. Preheat the Ninja Dual Zone Air Fryer to 180°C on zone 1 for 5 minutes.
4. Thread the marinated chicken, green bell pepper, and red onion onto skewers, alternating between each ingredient.
5. Place the skewers on the crisper plate in zone 1 and air fry at 180°C for 20 minutes or until the chicken is fully cooked and the vegetables are tender.
6. Once cooked, remove from the air fryer and serve immediately.

Moroccan Ras el Hanout Chicken Drumsticks

Prep Time: 10 minutes / Marination time: 1-2 hours / Cook time: 25 minutes / Serves: 4

Ingredients:

- 8 chicken drumsticks
- 2 tbsp ras el hanout spice blend
- 1 tbsp olive oil
- Salt and black pepper, to taste
- 1 lemon, sliced into wedges

Preparation Instructions:

1. In a bowl, mix together the ras el hanout spice blend, olive oil, salt, and black pepper.
2. Add the chicken drumsticks to the bowl, making sure they are well coated. Cover the bowl with plastic wrap and refrigerate for at least 1 hour or up to 2 hours.
3. Preheat the Ninja Dual Zone Air Fryer to 200°C on zone 1 for 5 minutes.
4. Place the marinated chicken drumsticks on the crisper plate in zone 1 and air fry at 200°C for 25 minutes or until the chicken is fully cooked and crispy.
5. Once cooked, remove from the air fryer and serve with lemon wedges on the side.

Chicken Fried Steak

Prep Time: 15 minutes / Cook time: 15 minutes / Serves: 4

Ingredients:

- 4 beef cube steaks (about 150g each)
- 120g all-purpose flour
- 2 tsp paprika
- 1 tsp garlic powder
- 1 tsp onion powder
- 1/2 tsp cayenne pepper
- Salt and black pepper, to taste
- 2 large eggs
- 60ml buttermilk
- Vegetable oil, for frying

Preparation Instructions:

1. Preheat the Ninja Dual Zone Air Fryer to 200°C on zone 1 for 5 minutes.
2. In a shallow dish, combine the all-purpose flour, paprika, garlic powder, onion powder, cayenne pepper, salt, and black pepper.
3. In a separate bowl, whisk together the eggs and buttermilk.
4. Dredge each beef cube steak in the flour mixture, coating it thoroughly. Shake off any excess flour.
5. Dip the coated steak into the egg and buttermilk mixture, allowing any excess to drip off.
6. Return the steak to the flour mixture and coat it again, pressing the flour mixture onto the steak to ensure a good coating.
7. Place the coated steaks in zone 1 of the air fryer and drizzle them with vegetable oil.
8. Cook the steaks at 200°C for 15 minutes, flipping them halfway through the cooking time, or until they are golden brown and cooked through.
9. Once cooked, remove the chicken fried steaks from the air fryer and let them rest on a wire rack for a few minutes to allow the coating to crisp up.
10. Serve the chicken fried steaks hot, accompanied by mashed potatoes, country gravy, and a side of steamed vegetables. Enjoy the crispy and flavorful goodness of this classic Southern dish.

Chicken Parmesan

Prep Time: 20 minutes / Cook time: 15 minutes / Serves: 4

Ingredients:

- 4 boneless, skinless chicken breasts
- 120g breadcrumbs
- 50g grated Parmesan cheese
- 1 tsp dried oregano
- 1/2 tsp garlic powder
- Salt and black pepper, to taste
- 2 large eggs, beaten
- 60ml milk
- 250g marinara sauce

- 150g shredded mozzarella cheese
- Fresh basil leaves, for garnish

Preparation Instructions:

1. Preheat the Ninja Dual Zone Air Fryer to 200°C on zone 1 for 5 minutes.
2. In a shallow dish, combine the breadcrumbs, grated Parmesan cheese, dried oregano, garlic powder, salt, and black pepper.
3. In a separate bowl, whisk together the beaten eggs and milk.
4. Dredge each chicken breast in the breadcrumb mixture, coating it thoroughly. Press the breadcrumbs onto the chicken to ensure a good coating.
5. Dip the coated chicken into the egg and milk mixture, allowing any excess to drip off.
6. Return the chicken to the breadcrumb mixture and coat it again, pressing the breadcrumbs onto the chicken to create a thick crust.
7. Place the coated chicken breasts in zone 1 of the air fryer and cook at 200°C for 15 minutes, or until they are cooked through and the crust is golden brown.
8. Once cooked, remove the chicken breasts from the air fryer and spoon marinara sauce over each breast.
9. Sprinkle the shredded mozzarella cheese on top of the sauce.
10. Return the chicken to the air fryer and cook for an additional 2-3 minutes, or until the cheese is melted and bubbly.
11. Once melted, remove the chicken Parmesan from the air fryer and garnish with fresh basil leaves.
12. Serve the chicken Parmesan hot, accompanied by spaghetti or your favourite pasta, and additional marinara sauce. Enjoy the delicious combination of crispy chicken, tangy sauce, and melted cheese in this classic Italian dish.

Buffalo Turkey Meatballs

Prep Time: 15 minutes / Cook time: 15 minutes / Serves: 4

Ingredients:

- 450g ground turkey
- 60g breadcrumbs
- 60g finely chopped onion
- 1 egg
- 60ml buffalo sauce
- 1/2 tsp garlic powder
- 1/2 tsp salt
- 1/4 tsp black pepper
- 1 tbsp olive oil

Preparation Instructions:

1. Preheat your Ninja Dual Zone Air Fryer to 190°C using the AIR FRY function.
2. In a mixing bowl, combine the ground turkey, breadcrumbs, onion, egg, buffalo sauce, garlic powder, salt, and black pepper.
3. Mix well until all Ingredients are thoroughly combined.
4. Form the mixture into 16 meatballs.
5. Brush the meatballs with olive oil to help brown and crisp in the air fryer.
6. Arrange the meatballs in a single layer on the crisper plate of the air fryer and place it in zone 1.
7. Select "AIR FRY" at 190°C for 15 minutes.
8. Select "SYNC" followed by the "START/STOP" button.
9. Serve hot with additional buffalo sauce for dipping.

Baked Pesto-Stuffed Chicken Breasts

Prep Time: 15 minutes / Cook time: 25 minutes / Serves: 2

Ingredients:

- 2 boneless, skinless chicken breasts
- 60g basil pesto
- 60g grated Parmesan cheese
- 1/4 tsp salt
- 1/4 tsp black pepper
- 1 tbsp olive oil

Preparation Instructions:

1. Preheat your Ninja Dual Zone Air Fryer to 190°C using the ROAST function.
2. Cut a pocket horizontally into the thickest part of each chicken breast, being careful not to cut through the other side.
3. In a small bowl, mix together the pesto, Parmesan cheese, salt, and black pepper.
4. Spoon the mixture evenly into the pockets of each chicken breast.
5. Brush the chicken breasts with olive oil.
6. Arrange the chicken breasts on the crisper plate of the air fryer and place it in zone 2.
7. Select "ROAST" at 190°C for 25 minutes.
8. Select "SYNC" followed by the "START/STOP" button.
9. Serve hot with a side of roasted vegetables or salad.

Chapter 5 Fish and Seafood

Skate with Capers

Prep Time: 15 minutes / Cook Time: 20 minutes / Servings: 4

Ingredients:

- 4 skate wings
- 2 tablespoons capers
- 2 cloves garlic, minced
- 1 lemon, juiced
- Salt and black pepper to taste
- 2 tablespoons olive oil

Preparation Instructions:

1. Preheat the Ninja Air Fryer to 375°F using the Air Fry mode.
2. In a bowl, combine the olive oil, capers, minced garlic, lemon juice, salt, and black pepper to make a marinade.
3. Place the skate wings in a shallow dish and pour the marinade over them. Ensure the skate wings are evenly coated. Cover and marinate for about 10 minutes.
4. Lightly coat the air fryer basket with cooking spray.
5. Place the marinated skate wings in the air fryer basket, making sure they are not overcrowded.
6. Air fry for about 15-20 minutes until the skate is cooked through and has a crispy exterior, turning them once during cooking.
7. Serve your Skate with Capers hot, drizzled with any remaining marinade.

Kipper and Potato Bake

Prep Time: 15 minutes / Cook Time: 40 minutes / Servings: 4

Ingredients:

- 4 kipper fillets
- 4 large potatoes, thinly sliced
- 1 onion, thinly sliced
- 250ml heavy cream
- 2 cloves garlic, minced
- 1 tablespoon fresh dill, chopped
- Salt and black pepper to taste

Preparation Instructions:

1. Preheat the Ninja Air Fryer to 375°F using the Bake mode.
2. In a bowl, mix the heavy cream, minced garlic, chopped dill, salt, and black pepper.
3. In a greased baking dish, layer the sliced potatoes and sliced onions.
4. Pour half of the cream mixture over the potato and onion layers.

5. Place the kipper fillets on top of the potato and onion layers.
6. Pour the remaining cream mixture over the kipper fillets.
7. Cover the baking dish with foil.
8. Place the baking dish in the air fryer basket.
9. Bake for about 35-40 minutes, removing the foil for the last 10 minutes, until the potatoes are tender and the kippers are cooked through.
10. Serve your Kipper and Potato Bake hot, garnished with extra dill.

Salmon and Spinach Stuffed Sole

Prep Time: 20 minutes / Cook Time: 20 minutes / Servings: 4

Ingredients:

- 4 sole fillets
- 200g (grams) salmon fillet, diced
- 150g fresh spinach, chopped
- 60ml heavy cream
- 2 cloves garlic, minced
- 1 lemon, zested and juiced
- Salt and black pepper to taste

Preparation Instructions:

1. Preheat the Ninja Air Fryer to 375°F using the Bake mode.
2. In a bowl, mix the diced salmon, chopped spinach, heavy cream, minced garlic, lemon zest, lemon juice, salt, and black pepper.
3. Lay the sole fillets flat on a clean surface and divide the salmon and spinach mixture evenly among them.
4. Roll up the sole fillets and secure with toothpicks.
5. Place the stuffed sole fillets in a baking dish.
6. Bake in the air fryer for about 20 minutes or until the fish is cooked through.

Whitebait Fritters

Prep Time: 15 minutes / Cook Time: 10 minutes / Servings: 4

Ingredients:

- 200g whitebait
- 60g all-purpose flour
- 1/2 teaspoon baking powder
- 1 egg
- 60ml milk
- Salt and black pepper to taste
- Cooking spray

Preparation Instructions:
1. Preheat the Ninja Air Fryer to 375°F using the Air Fry mode.
2. In a bowl, combine the all-purpose flour, baking powder, egg, milk, salt, and black pepper to make the batter.
3. Add the whitebait to the batter and mix until coated.
4. Lightly coat the air fryer basket with cooking spray to prevent sticking.
5. Drop spoonfuls of the whitebait mixture into the air fryer basket.
6. Air fry for about 10 minutes or until the whitebait fritters are golden and crispy.

Bass with Sauce Vierge

Ingredients:
- 4 bass fillets
- 240ml cherry tomatoes, halved
- 2 cloves garlic, minced
- 60 ml extra virgin olive oil
- 2 tablespoons fresh basil, chopped
- 1 lemon, zested and juiced
- Salt and black pepper to taste

Preparation Instructions:
1. Preheat the Ninja Air Fryer to 375°F using the Air Fry mode.
2. In a bowl, combine the halved cherry tomatoes, minced garlic, extra virgin olive oil (60 ml), chopped basil, lemon zest, lemon juice, salt, and black pepper to make the Sauce Vierge.
3. Season the bass fillets with salt and black pepper.
4. Place the bass fillets in the air fryer basket.
5. Air fry the bass fillets for about 15 minutes or until they are cooked through and have a crispy exterior.
6. Serve the Bass with Sauce Vierge, drizzling the Sauce Vierge over the fillets.

Monkfish with Parma Ham

Ingredients:
- 4 monkfish fillets
- 4 slices Parma ham
- 1 lemon, zested and juiced
- 30ml olive oil
- 15g fresh rosemary, chopped
- Salt and black pepper to taste

Preparation Instructions:
1. Preheat the Ninja Air Fryer to 375°F using the Air Fry mode.
2. Wrap each monkfish fillet with a slice of Parma ham.
3. In a bowl, combine the lemon zest, lemon juice, olive oil (30 ml), chopped fresh rosemary, salt, and black pepper.
4. Brush the monkfish fillets with the lemon and rosemary mixture.
5. Place the wrapped monkfish fillets in the air fryer basket.
6. Air fry the monkfish for about 15 minutes or until they are cooked through and the Parma ham is crispy.
7. Serve the Monkfish with Parma Ham hot, drizzled with any remaining lemon and rosemary mixture.

Lobster and Scallop Thermidor

Ingredients:
- 2 lobster tails, cooked and meat removed
- 12 large scallops
- 2 tablespoons butter
- 2 cloves garlic, minced
- 30 g grated Parmesan cheese
- 120 ml heavy cream
- 1 tablespoon Dijon mustard
- 1 teaspoon fresh tarragon, chopped
- Salt and black pepper to taste
- 30 g fresh breadcrumbs
- 2 tablespoons chopped fresh parsley

Preparation Instructions:
1. Preheat the Ninja Air Fryer to 375°F using the Air Fry mode.
2. Cut the lobster meat into bite-sized pieces and set aside.
3. In a saucepan, melt the butter over medium heat. Add the minced garlic and cook for about 1 minute until fragrant.
4. Stir in the grated Parmesan cheese, heavy cream, Dijon mustard, and fresh tarragon. Cook for another 3-4 minutes until the sauce thickens.
5. Season the sauce with salt and black pepper to taste.
6. Place the scallops in the air fryer basket and pour the sauce over them.
7. Air fry the scallops for about 10 minutes or until they are cooked through and the sauce is bubbling.
8. Top with fresh breadcrumbs and chopped parsley.
9. Air fry for an additional 5-7 minutes until the breadcrumbs are golden and crispy.
10. Serve the Lobster and Scallop Thermidor hot.

Monkfish Cheeks

Ingredients:
- 500g monkfish cheeks
- 60g flour

- 2 eggs, beaten   • 120g breadcrumbs
- 1 lemon, zested and juiced
- Salt and black pepper to taste

Preparation Instructions:

1. Preheat the Ninja Air Fryer to 375°F using the Air Fry mode.
2. Dredge the monkfish cheeks in flour, dip them in beaten eggs, and coat them with breadcrumbs.
3. Place the breaded monkfish cheeks in the air fryer basket.
4. Air fry for about 10 minutes, turning them halfway through, until they are golden and crispy.
5. In a small bowl, combine lemon zest, lemon juice, salt, and black pepper.
6. Drizzle the lemon mixture over the cooked monkfish cheeks.
7. Serve the Monkfish Cheeks hot.

Mussels in Cider

Prep Time: 15 minutes / Cook Time: 10 minutes / Servings: 4

Ingredients:

- 1kg mussels, cleaned and debearded
- 30g butter   • 1 onion, finely chopped
- 2 cloves garlic, minced
- 240ml dry cider   • 120ml heavy cream
- Fresh parsley, chopped, for garnish
- Salt and black pepper to taste

Preparation Instructions:

1. Preheat the Ninja Air Fryer to 375°F using the Air Fry mode.
2. In a large pan, melt the butter over medium heat. Add the finely chopped onion and minced garlic. Cook for about 2-3 minutes until they are soft and fragrant.
3. Pour in the dry cider and bring it to a simmer.
4. Add the cleaned mussels to the pan and cover with a lid. Cook for about 5-7 minutes or until the mussels have opened. Discard any mussels that do not open.
5. Stir in the heavy cream and season with salt and black pepper.
6. Place the mussels and sauce in the air fryer basket.
7. Air fry for an additional 3-4 minutes to heat through.
8. Serve the Mussels in Cider hot, garnished with chopped fresh parsley.

Sea Bass with Fennel and Blood Orange

Prep Time: 15 minutes / Cook Time: 15 minutes / Servings: 4

Ingredients:

- 4 sea bass fillets   • 2 fennel bulbs, thinly sliced

- 2 blood oranges, peeled and segmented
- 60ml olive oil
- 1 tablespoon fresh thyme leaves
- Salt and black pepper to taste

Preparation Instructions:

1. Preheat the Ninja Air Fryer to 375°F using the Air Fry mode.
2. In a large bowl, combine the thinly sliced fennel, blood orange segments, olive oil (60 ml), and fresh thyme leaves.
3. Season the sea bass fillets with salt and black pepper.
4. Place the seasoned sea bass fillets in the air fryer basket.
5. Spoon the fennel and blood orange mixture over the sea bass.
6. Air fry for about 12-15 minutes or until the sea bass is cooked through and the fennel is tender.
7. Serve the Sea Bass with Fennel and Blood Orange hot.

Hake and Chorizo Stew

Prep Time: 20 minutes / Cook Time: 20 minutes / Servings: 4 / Mode

Ingredients:

- 4 hake fillets
- 120g chorizo sausage, sliced
- 1 onion, finely chopped
- 2 cloves garlic, minced
- 400g canned chopped tomatoes
- 240 ml chicken broth
- 400g canned white beans, drained and rinsed
- 2 tablespoons fresh parsley, chopped
- Salt and black pepper to taste

Preparation Instructions:

1. Preheat the Ninja Air Fryer to 375°F using the Air Fry mode.
2. In a large pan, cook the sliced chorizo over medium heat until it releases its oil.
3. Add the finely chopped onion and minced garlic. Cook for about 3-4 minutes until they are soft and fragrant.
4. Stir in the canned chopped tomatoes and chicken broth. Simmer for about 5 minutes.
5. Add the drained white beans and chopped fresh parsley. Season with salt and black pepper.
6. Place the hake fillets in the air fryer basket.
7. Pour the chorizo and tomato mixture over the hake fillets.
8. Air fry for about 15-20 minutes or until the hake is cooked through.
9. Serve the Hake and Chorizo Stew hot, garnished with additional fresh parsley if desired.

Grilled Sardines

Prep Time: 10 minutes / Cook Time: 10 minutes / Servings: 4

Ingredients:

- 8 fresh sardines, cleaned and gutted
- 2 cloves garlic, minced
- 30ml olive oil   • Juice and zest of 1 lemon
- 2 tablespoons fresh parsley, chopped
- Salt and black pepper to taste

Preparation Instructions:

1. Preheat the Ninja Air Fryer to 375°F using the Air Fry mode.
2. In a bowl, combine the minced garlic, olive oil (30 ml), lemon juice, lemon zest, chopped fresh parsley, salt, and black pepper.
3. Brush the sardines with the lemon and garlic mixture.
4. Place the sardines in the air fryer basket.
5. Air fry the sardines for about 8-10 minutes or until they are cooked through and have crispy skin.
6. Serve the Grilled Sardines hot, drizzled with any remaining lemon and garlic mixture.

Plaice Goujons

Prep Time: 15 minutes / Cook Time: 10 minutes / Servings: 4

Ingredients:

- 4 plaice fillets, cut into strips
- 100g all-purpose flour   • 2 eggs, beaten
- 200g breadcrumbs   • 1 lemon, zested
- Salt and black pepper to taste
- Cooking spray or oil for air frying

Preparation Instructions:

1. Preheat the Ninja Air Fryer to 375°F using the Air Fry mode.
2. Dredge the plaice strips in flour, dip them in beaten eggs, and coat them with breadcrumbs mixed with lemon zest, salt, and black pepper.
3. Place the breaded plaice goujons in the air fryer basket.
4. Lightly spray with cooking spray or brush with oil to help them crisp up.
5. Air fry for about 8-10 minutes or until the plaice goujons are golden and crispy.
6. Serve the Plaice Goujons hot with your favorite dipping sauce.

Tuna Nicoise Salad

Prep Time: 15 minutes / Cook Time: 15 minutes / Servings: 4

Ingredients:

- 4 tuna steaks   • 200g green beans, trimmed
- 4 large eggs   • 200g cherry tomatoes
- 150g black olives   • 100g anchovy fillets
- 950g mixed salad greens
- 120ml olive oil   • 30ml red wine vinegar
- Salt and black pepper to taste

Preparation Instructions:

1. Preheat the Ninja Air Fryer to 375°F using the Air Fry mode.
2. Toss the green beans with olive oil, salt, and black pepper. Place them in the air fryer basket.
3. Air fry for about 8-10 minutes or until the green beans are tender and slightly crispy.
4. In a saucepan, place the eggs and cover with water. Bring to a boil, then reduce the heat and simmer for 8-10 minutes.
5. Cool the boiled eggs in cold water, peel them, and cut them into quarters.
6. Season the tuna steaks with salt and black pepper. Place them in the air fryer basket.
7. Air fry for about 6-8 minutes or until the tuna is cooked to your desired level.
8. In a large bowl, arrange the mixed salad greens, cherry tomatoes, black olives, and anchovy fillets.
9. Top with the air-fried green beans and tuna steaks.
10. In a small bowl, whisk together olive oil and red wine vinegar. Drizzle over the salad.
11. Serve the Tuna Nicoise Salad with the quartered boiled eggs as garnish.

Skate with Black Butter

Prep Time: 15 minutes / Cook Time: 10 minutes / Servings: 4

Ingredients:

- 4 skate wings, cleaned and trimmed
- 100g all-purpose flour
- 60g unsalted butter • Juice of 1 lemon
- 2 tablespoons fresh parsley, chopped
- Salt and black pepper to taste

Preparation Instructions:

1. Preheat the Ninja Air Fryer to 375°F using the Air Fry mode.
2. Season the skate wings with salt and black pepper.
3. Dredge the skate wings in all-purpose flour, shaking off any excess.
4. Place the skate wings in the air fryer basket.
5. Air fry for about 8-10 minutes, flipping halfway through, until the skate is cooked through and crispy.
6. While the skate is cooking, melt the unsalted butter in a small pan over low heat. Cook until it turns golden brown, then remove from heat.

7. Stir in the lemon juice and chopped fresh parsley into the browned butter.
8. Serve the air-fried Skate with Black Butter, drizzled with the lemon and parsley brown butter.

Seafood Paella

Prep Time: 20 minutes / Cook Time: 30 minutes / Servings: 4

Ingredients:

- 200g large shrimp, peeled and deveined
- 200g mussels, cleaned and debearded
- 200g squid rings
- 1 onion, chopped
- 2 cloves garlic, minced
- 200g Arborio rice
- 1 teaspoon smoked paprika
- 1/2 teaspoon saffron threads
- 800ml chicken broth
- 150g frozen peas
- 1 red bell pepper, sliced
- 2 tablespoons olive oil
- Salt and black pepper to taste
- Lemon wedges for garnish

Preparation Instructions:

1. Preheat the Ninja Air Fryer to 375°F using the Air Fry mode.
2. In a large ovenproof skillet, heat the olive oil over medium heat. Add the chopped onion and minced garlic. Sauté for about 2-3 minutes until they are soft and fragrant.
3. Stir in the Arborio rice, smoked paprika, and saffron threads. Cook for 2-3 minutes, stirring constantly.
4. Pour in the chicken broth and bring it to a simmer. Reduce the heat to low and cover with a lid. Cook for about 15 minutes until the rice is almost tender.
5. Arrange the seafood (shrimp, mussels, and squid rings), frozen peas, and sliced red bell pepper on top of the partially cooked rice.
6. Place the skillet in the air fryer and air fry for about 10-15 minutes until the seafood is cooked and the rice is tender.
7. Serve the Seafood Paella hot, garnished with lemon wedges.

Baked Gurnard with Tomato and Olives

Prep Time: 20 minutes / Cook Time: 15 minutes / Servings: 4

Ingredients:

- 4 gurnard fillets
- 400g cherry tomatoes, halved
- 100g green olives, pitted and sliced
- 2 cloves garlic, minced
- 1 tablespoon olive oil
- 2 tablespoons fresh basil, chopped
- Salt and black pepper to taste
- Lemon wedges for garnish

Preparation Instructions:

1. Preheat the Ninja Air Fryer to 375°F using the Air Fry mode.
2. In a bowl, combine the halved cherry tomatoes, sliced green olives, minced garlic, olive oil, chopped fresh basil, salt, and black pepper.
3. Lay out four large pieces of aluminum foil. Place a gurnard fillet in the centre of each piece of foil.
4. Spoon the tomato and olive mixture over each gurnard fillet.
5. Fold the foil over the fillets to create packets, sealing them tightly.
6. Place the foil packets in the air fryer basket.
7. Air fry for about 12-15 minutes, or until the fish is cooked through and the tomatoes are soft and slightly caramelised.
8. Serve the Baked Gurnard with Tomato and Olives in the foil packets, garnished with lemon wedges.

Dover Sole Meunière

Prep Time: 15 minutes / Cook Time: 10 minutes / Servings: 4

Ingredients:

- 4 Dover sole fillets
- 50g all-purpose flour
- 60g unsalted butter
- Juice of 1 lemon
- 2 tablespoons fresh parsley, chopped
- Salt and black pepper to taste

Preparation Instructions:

1. Preheat the Ninja Air Fryer to 375°F using the Air Fry mode.
2. Season the Dover sole fillets with salt and black pepper.
3. Dredge the fillets in all-purpose flour, shaking off any excess.
4. Place the Dover sole fillets in the air fryer basket.
5. Air fry for about 8-10 minutes, flipping halfway through, until the fillets are cooked through and crispy.
6. While the fish is cooking, melt the unsalted butter in a small pan over low heat. Cook until it turns golden brown, then remove from heat.
7. Stir in the lemon juice and chopped fresh parsley into the browned butter.
8. Serve the Dover Sole Meunière hot, drizzled with the lemon and parsley brown butter.

French Pan-Seared Scallops with Garlic Butter

Prep Time: 5 minutes / Cook time: 10 minutes / Servings: 2

Ingredients:

- 12 large sea scallops
- Salt and pepper, to taste
- 2 tbsp unsalted butter
- 2 garlic cloves, minced
- 1 tbsp chopped fresh parsley
- Lemon wedges, for serving

Preparation Instructions:

1. Season the scallops with salt and pepper.
2. Preheat the Ninja Dual Zone Air Fryer to 200°C on zone 1 for 5 minutes.
3. Add the butter to a skillet and place it in zone 2 of the air fryer to melt and heat up.
4. Add the minced garlic to the melted butter and cook for 1 minute until fragrant.
5. Add the scallops to the skillet and sear them for 2-3 minutes on each side until golden brown.
6. Remove the skillet from the air fryer and sprinkle the scallops with chopped parsley.
7. Serve the scallops immediately with lemon wedges on the side.

Korean Soy-Garlic Glazed Salmon

Prep Time: 10 minutes / Cook time: 15 minutes / Servings: 2

Ingredients:

- 2 salmon fillets, about 200g each
- 60ml soy sauce
- 3 tbsp brown sugar
- 1 tbsp sesame oil
- 3 cloves garlic, minced
- 1 tbsp grated ginger
- 1 tbsp mirin
- 1 tbsp rice vinegar
- 1 tbsp cornstarch
- 2 green onions, sliced
- sesame seeds, for garnish

Preparation Instructions:

1. Preheat the Ninja Dual Zone Air Fryer to 200°C on zone 1 for 5 minutes.
2. In a small bowl, whisk together the soy sauce, brown sugar, sesame oil, garlic, ginger, mirin, rice vinegar, and cornstarch.
3. Brush the salmon fillets with the glaze mixture on both sides.
4. Place the salmon fillets on the crisper plate in zone 1 and air fry at 200°C for 12-15 minutes or until the salmon is cooked through and the glaze is caramelised.
5. Once cooked, remove from the air fryer and sprinkle with sliced green onions and sesame seeds.
6. Serve immediately.

Crispy Air-Fried Calamari Rings

Prep Time: 30 minutes / Cook Time: 20 minutes / Servings: 2

Ingredients:

- 250 grams calamari rings
- 100 grams all-purpose flour
- 1 teaspoon paprika
- 1/2 teaspoon garlic powder
- 1/2 teaspoon salt   • 1/4 teaspoon black pepper
- 2 eggs   • Cooking spray or oil (for air frying)
- Lemon wedges (for serving)

Preparation Instructions:

1. Combine the all-purpose flour, paprika, garlic powder, salt, and black pepper in a shallow bowl. Mix well to create the coating mixture.
2. In a separate bowl, beat the eggs until well combined.
3. Dip the calamari rings into the beaten eggs, allow excess eggs drip off, then coat them in the flour mixture, pressing gently to ensure even coating. Repeat the process for all the calamari rings.
4. Preheat the air fryer to 200°C for about 5 minutes.
5. Lightly coat the air fryer drawer with cooking spray or brush it with oil to prevent sticking.
6. Arrange the coated calamari rings in a single layer in the air fryer non stick plates, ensuring they do not overlap.
7. Air fry the calamari rings at 200°C (400°F) for 8-10 minutes, flipping them halfway through, until they turn golden brown and crispy.
8. Once cooked, remove the crispy calamari rings from the air fryer and transfer them to a serving plate. Squeeze fresh lemon juice over the rings and serve.

Buffalo-style Air-Fried Shrimp

Prep Time: 120 minutes / Cook Time: 6 minutes / Servings: 2

Ingredients:

- 500 grams large shrimp, peeled and deveined
- 60 grams all-purpose flour
- 10 grams cornstarch • 1 teaspoon paprika
- 1/2 teaspoon garlic powder
- 60 ml hot sauce (such as Frank's RedHot
- 1/2 teaspoon salt   • 1/4 teaspoon black pepper
- 2 eggs)   • 60 grams butter, melted
- Cooking spray or oil (for air frying)
- Ranch or blue cheese dressing (for serving)
- Celery sticks (for serving)

Preparation Instructions:

1. Combine the all-purpose flour, cornstarch, paprika, garlic powder, salt, and black pepper in a shallow bowl. Mix well to create the coating mixture.

2. In a separate bowl, beat the eggs. In another bowl, combine the hot sauce and melted butter.
3. Dip the shrimp into the beaten eggs, allowing any excess to drip off, then coat them in the flour mixture, pressing gently to ensure even coating. Repeat the process for all the shrimp.
4. Preheat the Ninja Dual Zone Air Fryer to 200°C (400°F) for about 5 minutes.
5. Lightly coat the air fryer basket with cooking spray or brush it with oil to prevent sticking.
6. Place the coated shrimp in a single layer in the air fryer drawers, ensuring they do not overlap. Set the Dual Zone Air Fryer to Max Crisp mode.
7. Cook the shrimp in the first zone at 200°C (400°F) for 5 minutes.
8. While the first batch is cooking, lightly spray or brush the shrimp in the second zone with oil.
9. Once the first batch is done, transfer the cooked shrimp to a plate and cook the second batch in the second zone at 200°C (400°F) for 5 minutes.
10. Once all the shrimp are cooked, place them in a large bowl and pour the hot sauce and butter mixture over them. Toss the shrimp gently to ensure they are coated evenly.
11. Serve the buffalo-style air-fried shrimp immediately to savor the taste.

Beer-Battered Fish Tacos

Prep Time: 15 minutes / Cook time: 20 minutes / Serves: 4

Ingredients:
- 450g white fish fillets (cod or haddock)
- 250ml beer   • 1 large egg
- 200g plain flour
- 2 tsp baking powder
- 1 tsp smoked paprika
- 1/2 tsp cumin
- 1/2 tsp garlic powder
- 1/2 tsp onion powder
- 1/2 tsp sea salt
- 1/4 tsp black pepper
- 8 small flour tortillas
- 1 avocado, sliced
- 1/4 red cabbage, shredded
- 1 lime, cut into wedges
- 1 tbsp olive oil

Preparation Instructions:
1. Pat the fish fillets dry with a paper towel and cut them into small, taco-sized pieces.
2. In a bowl, whisk together the beer and egg until combined.
3. In a separate bowl, mix together the flour, baking powder, smoked paprika, cumin, garlic powder, onion powder, sea salt, and black pepper.
4. Pour the beer mixture into the flour mixture and whisk until smooth.
5. Dip each piece of fish into the batter, shaking off any excess.
6. Preheat the Ninja Dual Zone Air Fryer to 200°C using the "AIR FRY" function.
7. Place the battered fish in the crisper plate and spray with olive oil.
8. Select zone 1 and set the time to 10 minutes. Select "AIR FRY" at 200°C and press "START/STOP" to begin cooking.
9. While the fish cooks, warm the tortillas in the microwave or on a griddle.
10. When the fish is done, assemble the tacos by placing some shredded cabbage and avocado on each tortilla, then adding a few pieces of the fried fish on top. Serve with lime wedges.

Coconut-Crusted Mahi-Mahi

Prep Time: 10 minutes / Cook time: 12 minutes / Serves: 2

Ingredients:
- 2 mahi-mahi fillets
- 50g all-purpose flour
- 1 large egg, beaten
- 100g unsweetened shredded coconut
- 1/2 tsp sea salt
- 1/4 tsp black pepper
- 1 lime, cut into wedges
- 1 tbsp olive oil

Preparation Instructions:
1. Pat the mahi-mahi fillets dry with a paper towel.
2. Set up a breading station: place the flour in one shallow dish, the beaten egg in another dish, and the shredded coconut mixed with the sea salt and black pepper in a third dish.
3. Dip each fillet in the flour, shaking off any excess. Then, dip each fillet in the beaten egg, and finally coat each fillet with the coconut mixture.
4. Preheat the Ninja Dual Zone Air Fryer to 200°C using the "AIR FRY" function.
5. Place the coated mahi-mahi fillets in the crisper plate and spray with olive oil.
6. Select zone 1 and set the time to 6 minutes. Select "AIR FRY" at 200°C and press "START/STOP" to begin cooking.
7. When the timer goes off, carefully flip the fillets and cook for another 6 minutes.
8. Serve the coconut-crusted mahi-mahi with lime wedges on the side.

Chapter 6 Beef, Pork and Lamb

Beef and Spinach Timbales

Prep Time: 20 minutes / Cook Time: 25 minutes / Servings: 4

Ingredients:
- 300g ground beef
- 200g fresh spinach, chopped
- 1 small onion, finely chopped
- 2 cloves garlic, minced
- 2 tablespoons breadcrumbs
- 2 eggs
- 150ml heavy cream
- Salt and pepper to taste
- Butter for greasing

Preparation Instructions:
1. Preheat the Ninja Air Fryer to 375°F using the Bake mode.
2. In a pan, cook the ground beef, chopped onion, and minced garlic until the meat is browned and the onions are soft.
3. Add the chopped spinach and continue cooking until it wilts. Season with salt and pepper.
4. In a separate bowl, beat the eggs and heavy cream together.
5. Mix the breadcrumbs into the egg and cream mixture.
6. Grease individual ramekins or oven-safe dishes with butter.
7. Divide the beef and spinach mixture among the ramekins.
8. Pour the egg and cream mixture over the beef and spinach in each ramekin.
9. Place the ramekins in the air fryer basket.
10. Bake at 375°F for about 20-25 minutes, or until the timbales are set and golden.
11. Remove the Beef and Spinach Timbales from the air fryer and let them cool for a moment.
12. Serve the timbales hot.

Beef and caramelised Onion Tart

Prep Time: 20 minutes / Cook Time: 30 minutes / Servings: 4

Ingredients:
- 1 sheet of puff pastry
- 300g beef steak, thinly sliced
- 2 onions, thinly sliced
- 2 tablespoons olive oil
- 1 tablespoon brown sugar
- Salt and pepper to taste
- 100g cheddar cheese, grated
- Fresh thyme leaves for garnish

Preparation Instructions:
1. Preheat the Ninja Air Fryer to 375°F using the Bake mode.
2. Heat the olive oil in a pan over medium heat. Add the thinly sliced onions and cook until they become soft and caramelised, about 10-15 minutes. Sprinkle the brown sugar over the onions and continue to cook until caramelised. Set aside.
3. Roll out the puff pastry sheet and cut it into individual tart-sized portions.
4. Place the pastry portions on a greased air fryer tray or in the air fryer basket.
5. Spread the caramelised onions evenly over the pastry.
6. Layer the thinly sliced beef steak over the onions.
7. Season with salt and pepper.
8. Sprinkle the grated cheddar cheese over the beef.
9. Garnish with fresh thyme leaves.
10. Air fry at 375°F for about 20-30 minutes, or until the pastry is golden and the beef is cooked to your desired level.
11. Remove the Beef and caramelised Onion Tart from the air fryer and let it cool for a moment.
12. Serve the tart warm.

Beef and Wensleydale Pie

Prep Time: 30 minutes / Cook Time: 30 minutes / Servings: 4

Ingredients:
- 300g beef stewing meat, diced
- 1 onion, finely chopped
- 2 cloves garlic, minced
- 200ml beef broth
- 150g Wensleydale cheese, crumbled
- 1 sheet of shortcrust pastry
- 1 egg, beaten
- Salt and pepper to taste
- Butter for greasing

Preparation Instructions:
1. Preheat the Ninja Air Fryer to 375°F using the Bake mode.

2. In a pan, cook the diced beef until it's browned on all sides. Remove the beef and set it aside.
3. In the same pan, add the chopped onion and minced garlic. Cook until the onions are soft.
4. Return the browned beef to the pan and add beef broth. Simmer until the meat is tender.
5. Stir in the crumbled Wensleydale cheese, and season with salt and pepper.
6. Grease an oven-safe pie dish with butter.
7. Line the pie dish with the shortcrust pastry.
8. Pour the beef and Wensleydale mixture into the pastry-lined pie dish.
9. Place another pastry sheet on top and crimp the edges to seal.
10. Brush the top of the pie with beaten egg.
11. Place the pie dish in the air fryer basket.
12. Bake at 375°F for about 25-30 minutes, or until the pastry is golden brown.
13. Remove the Beef and Wensleydale Pie from the air fryer and let it cool for a moment.
14. Serve the pie hot.

Beef and Pea Pudding

Prep Time: 20 minutes / Cook Time: 45 minutes / Servings: 4

Ingredients:
- 300g ground beef
- 200g green peas
- 1 small onion, finely chopped
- 2 cloves garlic, minced
- 200g self-rising flour
- 100g suet
- 1/2 teaspoon dried thyme
- Salt and pepper to taste
- Butter for greasing

Preparation Instructions:
1. Preheat the Ninja Air Fryer to 375°F using the Bake mode.
2. In a pan, cook the ground beef, chopped onion, and minced garlic until the meat is browned and the onions are soft.
3. Stir in the green peas and dried thyme. Season with salt and pepper. Remove from heat.
4. In a bowl, combine the self-rising flour and suet. Add enough water to form a soft dough.
5. Roll out the dough on a floured surface to a rectangular shape.
6. Place the cooked beef and pea mixture over the dough.
7. Roll up the dough with the filling, sealing the edges.
8. Grease an oven-safe dish with butter and place the

pudding in it.
9. Bake at 375°F for about 40-45 minutes, or until the pudding is cooked and golden.
10. Remove the Beef and Pea Pudding from the air fryer and let it cool for a moment.
11. Serve the pudding hot.

Beef and Tattie Scones

Prep Time: 15 minutes / Cook Time: 15 minutes / Servings: 4

Ingredients:
- 300g mashed potatoes
- 200g ground beef
- 1 small onion, finely chopped
- 2 cloves garlic, minced
- 200g self-rising flour
- 100g butter, cold and diced
- 1/2 teaspoon dried rosemary
- Salt and pepper to taste
- Milk for brushing

Preparation Instructions:
1. Preheat the Ninja Air Fryer to 375°F using the Bake mode.
2. In a pan, cook the ground beef, chopped onion, and minced garlic until the meat is browned and the onions are soft.
3. Stir in the dried rosemary. Season with salt and pepper. Remove from heat.
4. In a large bowl, combine the mashed potatoes and self-rising flour.
5. Add the cold diced butter and rub it into the mixture until it resembles breadcrumbs.
6. Add a little milk and continue to mix until the dough comes together.
7. Roll out the dough on a floured surface to about 1/2-inch thickness.
8. Cut the dough into scones or rounds.
9. Place a spoonful of the cooked beef mixture in the centre of each scone.
10. Fold the scones over to enclose the filling and press the edges to seal.
11. Place the scones on a greased air fryer tray or in the air fryer basket.
12. Brush the tops of the scones with a little milk.
13. Bake at 375°F for about 10-15 minutes, or until the scones are golden and cooked through.
14. Remove the Beef and Tattie Scones from the air fryer and serve hot.

Pork and Prune Tagine

Prep Time: 20 minutes / Cook Time: 55 minutes / Servings: 4

Ingredients:

- 500g pork shoulder, diced
- 1 onion, chopped
- 2 cloves garlic, minced
- 200g prunes
- 1 teaspoon ground cinnamon
- 1 teaspoon ground cumin
- 1 teaspoon ground coriander
- 1 tablespoon honey
- 250ml chicken broth
- Salt and pepper to taste
- Fresh cilantro for garnish

Preparation Instructions:

1. Preheat the Ninja Air Fryer to 375°F using the Roast mode.
2. In a large ovenproof casserole dish, heat a little oil over medium heat.
3. Add the diced pork shoulder and brown on all sides. Remove the pork and set it aside.
4. In the same dish, add the chopped onion and minced garlic. Cook until the onions are soft.
5. Stir in the ground cinnamon, cumin, and coriander.
6. Return the browned pork to the dish.
7. Add the prunes, honey, and chicken broth.
8. Season with salt and pepper.
9. Cover the dish and place it in the air fryer.
10. Roast at 375°F for about 1 hour, or until the pork is tender.
11. Remove the Pork and Prune Tagine from the air fryer.
12. Garnish with fresh cilantro and serve hot.

Pork and Thyme Gratin

Prep Time: 20 minutes / Cook Time: 35 minutes / Servings: 4

Ingredients:

- 400g pork tenderloin, sliced
- 1 onion, finely chopped
- 2 cloves garlic, minced
- 2 tablespoons fresh thyme leaves
- 200ml heavy cream
- 200ml chicken broth
- 200g potatoes, thinly sliced
- 200g Gruyère cheese, grated
- Salt and pepper to taste
- Butter for greasing

Preparation Instructions:

1. Preheat the Ninja Air Fryer to 375°F using the Bake mode.
2. In a large pan, heat a little butter over medium heat.
3. Add the sliced pork tenderloin and cook until it's

browned. Remove the pork and set it aside.
4. In the same pan, add the chopped onion and minced garlic. Cook until the onions are soft.
5. Stir in the fresh thyme leaves and cook for another minute.
6. Pour in the heavy cream and chicken broth. Bring to a simmer and cook for a few minutes until the mixture thickens.
7. Season with salt and pepper to taste.
8. Grease an oven-safe dish with butter and layer the sliced potatoes at the bottom.
9. Place the cooked pork over the potatoes.
10. Pour the creamy mixture over the pork and potatoes.
11. Top the gratin with the grated Gruyère cheese.
12. Bake at 375°F for about 30-35 minutes, or until the potatoes are tender and the gratin is golden and bubbly.
13. Remove the Pork and Thyme Gratin from the air fryer and let it cool slightly before serving.

Pork and Chorizo Cassoulet

Prep Time: 20 minutes / Cook Time: 40 minutes / Servings: 4

Ingredients:

- 300g pork shoulder, diced
- 150g chorizo sausage, sliced
- 1 onion, chopped
- 2 cloves garlic, minced
- 2 cans (400g each) cannellini beans, drained and rinsed
- 400ml chicken broth
- 2 tablespoons tomato paste
- 1 teaspoon dried thyme
- 1 teaspoon paprika
- Salt and pepper to taste

Preparation Instructions:

1. Preheat the Ninja Air Fryer to 375°F using the Roast mode.
2. In a large ovenproof casserole dish, heat a little oil over medium heat.
3. Add the diced pork shoulder and brown on all sides. Remove the pork and set it aside.
4. In the same dish, add the sliced chorizo sausage and cook until it's browned. Remove the chorizo and set it aside.
5. Add the chopped onion and minced garlic. Cook until the onions are soft.
6. Return the browned pork and chorizo to the dish.
7. Stir in the cannellini beans, chicken broth, tomato paste, dried thyme, paprika, salt, and pepper.
8. Cover the dish and place it in the air fryer.

9. Roast at 375°F for about 35-40 minutes, or until the cassoulet is hot and bubbling.
10. Remove the Pork and Chorizo Cassoulet from the air fryer and let it cool slightly before serving.

Lamb and Roasted Pepper Quiche

Prep Time: 20 minutes / Cook Time: 40 minutes / Servings: 4

Ingredients:
- 300g ground lamb
- 1 red bell pepper, roasted, peeled, and diced
- 1 onion, finely chopped
- 2 cloves garlic, minced
- 4 large eggs
- 200ml heavy cream
- 100g feta cheese, crumbled
- 1 teaspoon dried oregano
- Salt and pepper to taste
- 1 pre-made pie crust

Preparation Instructions:
1. Preheat the Ninja Air Fryer to 375°F using the Bake mode.
2. In a large pan, cook the ground lamb over medium heat until it's browned. Remove any excess fat.
3. Add the chopped onion and minced garlic. Cook until the onions are soft.
4. In a bowl, whisk together the eggs, heavy cream, dried oregano, salt, and pepper.
5. Place the pre-made pie crust in a greased oven-safe dish.
6. Spread the cooked lamb and roasted red bell pepper over the pie crust.
7. Sprinkle the crumbled feta cheese over the lamb and pepper.
8. Pour the egg and cream mixture over the lamb and pepper.
9. Bake at 375°F for about 35-40 minutes, or until the quiche is set and the top is golden.
10. Remove the Lamb and Roasted Pepper Quiche from the air fryer and let it cool slightly before serving.

Lamb and caramelised Onion Gravy

Prep Time: 15 minutes / Cook Time: 30 minutes / Servings: 4

Ingredients:
- 400g lamb chops
- 2 onions, thinly sliced
- 2 cloves garlic, minced
- 2 tablespoons olive oil
- 1 tablespoon butter
- 1 tablespoon all-purpose flour
- 300ml beef broth
- 1 tablespoon Worcestershire sauce
- Salt and pepper to taste

Preparation Instructions:
1. Preheat the Ninja Air Fryer to 375°F using the Roast mode.
2. In a large ovenproof casserole dish, heat the olive oil and butter over medium heat.
3. Season the lamb chops with salt and pepper and brown them on both sides. Remove the lamb and set it aside.
4. In the same dish, add the sliced onions and minced garlic. Cook until the onions are caramelised.
5. Sprinkle the all-purpose flour over the onions and stir to combine.
6. Pour in the beef broth and Worcestershire sauce. Stir until the mixture thickens.
7. Return the browned lamb chops to the dish.
8. Cover the dish and place it in the air fryer.
9. Roast at 375°F for about 25-30 minutes, or until the lamb is tender and the gravy is rich and flavorful.
10. Remove the Lamb and caramelised Onion Gravy from the air fryer and serve hot.

Lamb and Tomato Tarts

Prep Time: 20 minutes / Cook Time: 30 minutes / Servings: 4

Ingredients:
- 400g ground lamb
- 1 onion, finely chopped
- 2 cloves garlic, minced
- 2 tomatoes, sliced
- 200ml heavy cream
- 4 pre-made tart shells
- 100g feta cheese, crumbled
- 2 tablespoons fresh basil leaves
- Salt and pepper to taste

Preparation Instructions:
1. Preheat the Ninja Air Fryer to 375°F using the Bake mode.
2. In a large pan, cook the ground lamb over medium heat until it's browned. Remove any excess fat.
3. Add the chopped onion and minced garlic. Cook until the onions are soft.
4. Season the lamb mixture with salt and pepper.
5. In a bowl, combine the cooked lamb, heavy cream, and crumbled feta cheese.
6. Spoon the lamb mixture into the pre-made tart shells.
7. Top each tart with slices of tomato.
8. Bake at 375°F for about 25-30 minutes, or until the

tarts are set and golden.

9. Remove the Lamb and Tomato Tarts from the air fryer and sprinkle fresh basil leaves on top before serving.

Beef and Horseradish Suet Pudding

Prep Time: 20 minutes / Cook Time 55 minutes / Servings: 4

Ingredients:

- 400g stewing beef, diced
- 2 onions, chopped
- 2 cloves garlic, minced
- 200g self-raising flour
- 100g beef suet
- 2 tablespoons horseradish sauce
- 200ml beef broth
- Salt and pepper to taste

Preparation Instructions:

1. Preheat the Ninja Air Fryer to 375°F using the Bake mode.
2. In a large ovenproof dish, combine the diced stewing beef, chopped onions, and minced garlic.
3. Season with salt and pepper.
4. In a mixing bowl, combine the self-raising flour, beef suet, and horseradish sauce.
5. Gradually add the beef broth and mix until a dough forms.
6. Roll out the dough to fit the top of the beef mixture in the dish.
7. Place the dough on top of the beef mixture, sealing the edges.
8. Bake at 375°F for about 55-60 minutes, or until the suet pudding is cooked through and golden.
9. Remove the Beef and Horseradish Suet Pudding from the air fryer and let it cool slightly before serving.

Pork and Brown Sauce Sandwich

Prep Time: 10 minutes / Cook Time: 15 minutes / Servings: 4

Ingredients:

- 400g cooked pork slices
- 4 sandwich buns
- 4 tablespoons brown sauce (HP Sauce or your favorite brown sauce)
- Lettuce leaves
- Sliced tomatoes
- Sliced onions

Preparation Instructions:

1. Preheat the Ninja Air Fryer to 375°F using the Roast mode.

2. Slice the sandwich buns in half and lightly toast them in the air fryer for a couple of minutes.
3. Spread brown sauce on the bottom half of each bun.
4. Layer the cooked pork slices on top of the brown sauce.
5. Add lettuce leaves, sliced tomatoes, and sliced onions.
6. Place the top half of the buns on the sandwich.
7. Roast the assembled Pork and Brown Sauce Sandwiches in the air fryer for about 5-7 minutes to heat through.
8. Remove the sandwiches from the air fryer and serve hot.

Pork and Date Stuffing

Prep Time: 15 minutes / Cook Time: 30 minutes / Servings: 4

Ingredients:

- 200g ground pork
- 1 onion, chopped
- Fresh breadcrumbs
- Chopped dates
- Chopped fresh parsley
- Chopped fresh sage
- Chicken broth
- Salt and pepper to taste

Preparation Instructions:

1. Preheat the Ninja Air Fryer to 375°F using the Bake mode.
2. In a large skillet, cook the ground pork and chopped onion until the pork is browned and the onion is soft. Remove any excess fat.
3. In a mixing bowl, combine the cooked pork and onion, fresh breadcrumbs, chopped dates, chopped fresh parsley, and chopped fresh sage.
4. Season with salt and pepper.
5. Gradually add the chicken broth to moisten the mixture, but don't make it too wet.
6. Transfer the stuffing mixture to a greased ovenproof dish.
7. Bake at 375°F for about 25-30 minutes, or until the stuffing is heated through and has a golden top.
8. Remove the Pork and Date Stuffing from the air fryer and serve as a side dish.

Filipino Fried Pork (Pritong Baboy)

Prep Time: 15 minutes / Cook Time: 20 minutes / Servings: 4

Ingredients:

- 500g pork belly, thinly sliced into bite-sized pieces

- Cooking spray
- 60ml soy sauce
- 60ml vinegar
- 1 onion, minced
- 4 cloves garlic, minced
- 1 bay leaf
- Salt and black pepper to taste

Preparation Instructions:

1. In a bowl, combine the soy sauce, vinegar, minced garlic, minced onion, bay leaf, salt, and black pepper to make the marinade.
2. Place the thinly sliced pork belly in a shallow dish and pour the marinade over it. Ensure the pork is evenly coated. Cover and marinate for at least 15 minutes, or longer for a more flavorful result.
3. Preheat the Ninja Air Fryer to 375°F using the Air Fry mode.
4. Lightly coat the air fryer basket with cooking spray to prevent sticking.
5. Once the air fryer is preheated, carefully arrange the marinated pork belly pieces in the basket, ensuring they are not overcrowded.
6. Air fry the pork at 375°F for about 8-10 minutes or until it's crispy and golden brown, turning them halfway through for even cooking.
7. Use tongs to remove the fried pork from the air fryer basket and place it on a plate lined with paper towels to drain excess oil.
8. Serve your Filipino Fried Pork hot, commonly enjoyed with steamed rice and a dipping sauce, such as vinegar with soy sauce and garlic.

Cajun Pork Fillet with Sweet Potatoes

Prep Time: 15 minutes / Cook Time: 25 minutes / Servings: 4

Ingredients:

- For the Cajun Pork Fillet:
- 4 pork fillets
- 2 tablespoons Cajun seasoning
- 2 tablespoons olive oil
- Salt and black pepper to taste
- For the Sweet Potatoes:
- 4 sweet potatoes, peeled and cubed
- 2 tablespoons olive oil
- 1 tablespoon paprika
- 1 teaspoon garlic powder
- 1 teaspoon onion powder
- Salt and black pepper to taste

Preparation Instructions:

Cajun Pork Fillet:

1. Preheat the Ninja Air Fryer to 375°F using the Air Fry mode.
2. In a bowl, combine the Cajun seasoning, olive oil, salt, and black pepper to make a marinade.
3. Rub the marinade over the pork fillets, ensuring they are evenly coated.
4. Place the pork fillets in the air fryer basket.
5. Air fry for about 20-25 minutes, turning them halfway through, until the pork is cooked through and has a nice crust.

Sweet Potatoes:

1. In a separate bowl, combine the cubed sweet potatoes, olive oil, paprika, garlic powder, onion powder, salt, and black pepper.
2. Toss the sweet potatoes to coat them in the seasoning.
3. Place the seasoned sweet potatoes in the air fryer basket, next to the pork fillets.
4. Air fry for about 20-25 minutes, or until the sweet potatoes are tender and slightly crispy.
5. Serve your Cajun Pork Fillet with Sweet Potatoes hot for the best feeling.

Tikka Pork Chops

Prep Time: 15 minutes /Cook Time: 20 minutes / Servings: 4

Ingredients:

- 4 boneless pork chops
- 250ml plain yoghurt
- 2 tablespoons tikka masala paste
- 2 cloves garlic, minced
- 1 tablespoon ginger, grated
- 1 teaspoon ground cumin
- 1 teaspoon ground coriander
- 1 teaspoon paprika
- Salt and black pepper to taste
- 2 tablespoons vegetable oil

Preparation Instructions:

1. In a bowl, combine the plain yoghurt, tikka masala paste, minced garlic, grated ginger, ground cumin, ground coriander, paprika, salt, and black pepper to make the marinade.
2. Place the boneless pork chops in a shallow dish and coat them with the marinade. Make sure the pork chops are evenly coated. Cover and refrigerate for at least 1 hour to marinate.
3. Preheat the Ninja Air Fryer to 375°F using the Air Fry mode.
4. Remove the marinated pork chops from the refrigerator and let them come to room temperature.
5. Brush the air fryer basket with 2 tablespoons of vegetable oil to prevent sticking.

6. Place the pork chops in the air fryer basket.
7. Air fry for about 18-20 minutes, turning them halfway through, until the pork is cooked through and has a nice char.
8. Serve your Tikka Pork Chops hot with your favorite side dishes.

Balsamic Pork with Apples

Prep Time: 15 minutes / Cook Time: 25 minutes / Servings: 4

Ingredients:
- 4 boneless pork chops
- 480 ml balsamic vinegar
- 30ml honey
- 2 cloves garlic, minced
- 5g dried thyme
- Salt and black pepper to taste
- 30 ml olive oil
- 2 apples, cored and sliced

Preparation Instructions:
1. Preheat the Ninja Air Fryer to 375°F using the Air Fry mode.
2. In a small bowl, whisk together the 480 ml of balsamic vinegar, 30 ml of honey, minced garlic, 5 g of dried thyme, salt, and black pepper to make the balsamic glaze.
3. Season the boneless pork chops with salt and black pepper.
4. Brush the pork chops with the balsamic glaze.
5. In a large mixing bowl, toss the sliced apples with 30 ml of olive oil and a pinch of salt.
6. Place the pork chops in the air fryer basket.
7. Arrange the apple slices around the pork chops.
8. Air fry for about 20-25 minutes, turning the pork chops and stirring the apples halfway through, until the pork is cooked through and the apples are tender.
9. Drizzle the remaining balsamic glaze over the cooked pork and apples.
10. Serve your delicious Balsamic Pork with Apples hot and enjoy.

Spanish Patatas Bravas and Chorizo Hash with Fried Eggs

Prep Time: 10 minutes / Cook time: 20 minutes / Serves: 2-4

Ingredients:
- 4 large potatoes, peeled and cut into bite-sized pieces
- 120g diced chorizo
- 1/2 onion, diced
- 1 red pepper, diced
- 2 cloves garlic, minced
- 1/2 tsp smoked paprika
- Salt and black pepper, to taste
- 4 eggs
- 60g chopped fresh parsley

Preparation Instructions:
1. Preheat the Ninja Dual Zone Air Fryer to 200°C on zone 1 for 5 minutes.
2. In a bowl, toss the potatoes with a little bit of oil and salt.
3. Place the potatoes on the crisper plate in zone 1 and air fry at 200°C for 15-20 minutes or until golden and crispy. Shake the basket halfway through cooking.
4. In a skillet, cook the chorizo over medium-high heat until crispy. Remove the chorizo from the skillet and set aside.
5. In the same skillet, cook the onion and red pepper until softened. Add the garlic and smoked paprika and cook for another minute.
6. Add the cooked potatoes to the skillet and toss with the vegetables. Add the cooked chorizo and toss again. Season with salt and black pepper to taste.
7. In another skillet, fry the eggs to your desired doneness.
8. Divide the potato and chorizo hash among 2-4 plates, depending on how many Servings you want. Top each serving with a fried egg and sprinkle with fresh parsley.

Indian Tandoori Lamb Chops with Mint Chutney

Prep Time: 20 minutes / Cook time: 10 minutes / Serves: 4

Ingredients:
- 8 lamb chops
- 120g plain yoghurt
- 2 tbsp tandoori spice mix
- 1 tbsp lemon juice
- Salt, to taste
- 60g chopped fresh mint
- 60g chopped fresh cilantro
- 2 green chilies, chopped
- 1 tsp grated ginger
- 1 tbsp lemon juice
- Salt, to taste

Preparation Instructions:
1. In a large bowl, mix together the yoghurt, tandoori spice mix, 1 tablespoon of lemon juice, and salt to

taste.

2. Add the lamb chops to the marinade and toss to coat. Let the lamb marinate for at least 1 hour, or overnight in the refrigerator.

3. Preheat the Ninja Dual Zone Air Fryer to 200°C on zone 1 for 5 minutes.

4. Remove the lamb chops from the marinade and place them on the crisper plate in zone 1 of the air fryer. Air fry for 10 minutes, or until the lamb chops are cooked to your desired level of doneness.

5. While the lamb chops are cooking, prepare the mint chutney by combining the mint, cilantro, green chilies, ginger, 1 tablespoon of lemon juice, and salt to taste in a food processor. Pulse until the mixture is finely chopped.

6. Serve the lamb chops with the mint chutney on the side.

Jamaican Beef Patty

Prep Time: 30 minutes / Cook time: 20 minutes / Serves: 4

Ingredients:

- For the pastry:
- 250g all-purpose flour
- 1/2 tsp turmeric powder (optional, for colour)
- 1/2 tsp salt
- 115g unsalted butter, cold and cubed
- 60ml ice water
- For the filling:
- 300g ground beef
- 1 small onion, finely chopped
- 1 clove garlic, minced
- 1 small carrot, finely grated
- 1 small potato, finely grated
- 2 tbsp vegetable oil
- 1 tsp curry powder
- 1/2 tsp dried thyme
- 1/4 tsp ground allspice
- Salt and black pepper, to taste
- 60ml beef or vegetable broth

Preparation Instructions:

1. Preheat the Ninja Dual Zone Air Fryer to 180°C on zone 1 for 5 minutes.

2. In a large bowl, combine the all-purpose flour, turmeric powder (if using), and salt for the pastry.

3. Add the cold cubed butter to the flour mixture and use your fingers or a pastry cutter to cut the butter into the flour until it resembles coarse crumbs.

4. Gradually add the ice water, a few tablespoons at a time, and mix until the dough comes together. Be careful not to overmix.

5. Shape the dough into a disk, wrap it in plastic wrap,

and refrigerate for at least 15 minutes.

6. While the dough is chilling, prepare the filling. In a pan, heat the vegetable oil over medium heat.

7. Add the chopped onion and minced garlic to the pan and sauté for 2-3 minutes, until they are softened and aromatic.

8. Add the ground beef to the pan and cook until it is browned and cooked through.

9. Stir in the grated carrot, grated potato, curry powder, dried thyme, ground allspice, salt, black pepper, and beef or vegetable broth. Cook for an additional 5 minutes, or until the vegetables are tender and the flavours have melded together.

10. Remove the filling from the heat and let it cool slightly.

11. Remove the chilled dough from the refrigerator and roll it out on a floured surface to a thickness of about 3-4 mm.

12. Use a round cutter or a glass to cut circles from the rolled-out dough. The circles should be about 12-15 cm in diameter.

13. Place a spoonful of the cooled filling onto one half of each dough circle, leaving a small border around the edges.

14. Fold the other half of the dough circle over the filling and press the edges together to seal. You can use a fork to crimp the edges for a decorative touch.

15. Place the Jamaican beef patties in zone 1 of the air fryer, ensuring they are not overcrowded.

16. Air fry the patties at 180°C for 15-20 minutes, or until they are golden brown and cooked through.

17. Once cooked, remove the beef patties from the air fryer and let them cool for a few minutes before serving.

18. Serve the Jamaican beef patties warm or at room temperature, and enjoy the deliciously spiced and savoury flavours of this classic Jamaican dish.

BBQ Pulled Pork Sliders

Prep Time: 10 minutes / Cook time: 35 minutes / Serves: 4-6

Ingredients:

- For the pork:
- 1. 5 kg pork shoulder
- 2 tbsp smoked paprika
- 1 tbsp garlic powder
- 1 tbsp onion powder
- 1 tbsp brown sugar
- 1 tbsp sea salt
- 1 tsp ground black pepper
- 250ml BBQ sauce

- For the sliders:
- 12 slider buns
- 1 small red onion, thinly sliced
- 1 small cucumber, thinly sliced
- 1 avocado, sliced
- 1 tbsp olive oil
- Sea salt and ground black pepper, to taste

Preparation Instructions:

1. Preheat the Ninja Dual Zone Air Fryer to 180°C on the Roast function.
2. Combine smoked paprika, garlic powder, onion powder, brown sugar, sea salt, and black pepper in a small bowl.
3. Rub the spice mixture all over the pork shoulder, making sure to coat it evenly.
4. Place the pork shoulder in zone 1 of the Air Fryer and roast for 20 minutes.
5. After 20 minutes, transfer the pork shoulder to zone 2 of the Air Fryer and roast for an additional 15 minutes.
6. Pour the BBQ sauce over the pork shoulder, making sure to coat it evenly.
7. Roast for an additional 10 minutes, or until the internal temperature reaches 71°C.
8. Once cooked, remove the pork shoulder from the Air Fryer and shred it with two forks.
9. In a separate bowl, toss the sliced red onion and cucumber with olive oil, salt, and black pepper.
10. To assemble the sliders, place a generous amount of pulled pork on each bun, top with the sliced avocado and the red onion and cucumber mixture.

Dehydrated Venison Jerky

Prep Time: 10 minutes / Cook time: 4-6 hours / Serves: 4

Ingredients:

- 500g venison, thinly sliced
- 120ml soy sauce
- 60ml Worcestershire sauce
- 60g brown sugar
- 1 teaspoon garlic powder
- 1 teaspoon onion powder
- 1/2 teaspoon smoked paprika
- 1/2 teaspoon black pepper

Preparation Instructions:

1. In a bowl, mix together soy sauce, Worcestershire

sauce, brown sugar, garlic powder, onion powder, smoked paprika, and black pepper. Add venison slices, and coat them with the mixture. Cover and refrigerate for at least 4 hours, or overnight.
2. Preheat the Ninja Dual Zone Air Fryer to 70°C for dehydrating.
3. Remove venison slices from the marinade, and pat them dry using paper towels. Arrange the venison slices on the dehydrator racks.
4. Select zone 1 and pair it with "DEHYDRATE" for 4-6 hours. Check the jerky after 4 hours and remove any pieces that are ready, then continue to dehydrate until the remaining jerky reaches your desired texture.
5. Once the jerky is done, remove it from the dehydrator and let it cool completely. Store in an airtight container at room temperature for up to 2 weeks.

Baked Bone Marrow

Prep Time: 10 minutes / Cook time: 20 minutes / Serves: 4

Ingredients:

- 4 bone marrow pieces (2-3 inches in length)
- 1 tsp sea salt
- 1/2 tsp black pepper
- 1 tsp fresh thyme leaves
- 1 garlic clove, minced
- 4 slices of crusty bread
- 1 tbsp olive oil

Preparation Instructions:

1. Preheat the Ninja Dual Zone Air Fryer to 200°C on the "ROAST" function.
2. Place the bone marrow pieces on a baking tray, sprinkle with sea salt, black pepper, thyme leaves, and minced garlic.
3. Roast the bone marrow for 20 minutes in zone 1 of the air fryer.
4. Meanwhile, brush the bread slices with olive oil and place them on the crisper plate in zone 2 of the air fryer.
5. Fry the bread slices for 5 minutes on the "AIR FRY" function until golden brown.
6. Serve the roasted bone marrow hot with the toasted bread slices.

Chapter 7 Snacks and Appetizers

Bannock Bread

Prep Time: 10 minutes / Cook Time: 20 minutes / Servings: 4

Ingredients:
- 200g all-purpose flour
- 1 tsp baking powder
- 1/2 tsp salt
- 100ml water

Preparation Instructions:
1. Preheat the Ninja Air Fryer to 375°F using the Bake mode.
2. In a mixing bowl, combine the all-purpose flour, baking powder, and salt.
3. Gradually add the water and knead the mixture until you have a smooth dough.
4. Roll out the dough into a round flatbread.
5. Place the bannock in the air fryer.
6. Bake for about 10 minutes, then flip and bake for an additional 10 minutes, or until the bread is golden brown and cooked through.
7. Remove the bannock from the air fryer and let it cool slightly before serving.

Corned Beef Hash Cakes

Prep Time: 15 minutes / Cook Time: 20 minutes / Servings: 4

Ingredients:
- 200g cooked corned beef, diced
- 200g cooked potatoes, mashed
- 100g onions, chopped
- 1/2 tsp dried thyme
- Salt and pepper to taste
- Cooking spray

Preparation Instructions:
1. Preheat the Ninja Air Fryer to 375°F using the Air Fry mode.
2. In a mixing bowl, combine the diced corned beef, mashed potatoes, chopped onions, dried thyme, salt, and pepper.
3. Form the mixture into small cakes or patties.
4. Lightly coat the hash cakes with cooking spray.
5. Place the hash cakes in the air fryer basket.
6. Air fry for about 15-20 minutes, flipping them halfway through, until they are golden and crispy.
7. Serve the Corned Beef Hash Cakes hot.

Venison Pasty

Prep Time: 20 minutes / Cook Time: 30 minutes / Servings: 4

Ingredients:
- 200g venison, diced
- 100g potatoes, diced
- 100g onions, chopped
- 100g carrots, diced
- 200g all-purpose flour
- 100g cold butter, diced
- 4-6 tbsp cold water
- Salt and pepper to taste
- Egg wash (1 beaten egg mixed with a little water)

Preparation Instructions:
1. Preheat the Ninja Air Fryer to 375°F using the Bake mode.
2. In a mixing bowl, combine the diced venison, potatoes, chopped onions, and diced carrots. Season with salt and pepper.
3. In a separate bowl, make the pastry by rubbing the cold butter into the all-purpose flour until it resembles breadcrumbs. Gradually add cold water and mix until the pastry comes together.
4. Roll out the pastry and cut it into circles.
5. Place a portion of the venison and vegetable mixture onto each pastry circle.
6. Fold the pastry over the filling to create a semi-circle and crimp the edges to seal.
7. Brush the pasties with egg wash.
8. Bake in the air fryer for about 25-30 minutes or until the pasties are golden and the filling is cooked.
9. Let the Venison Pasty cool for a few minutes before serving.

Angels on Horseback

Prep Time: 15 minutes / Cook Time: 5 minutes / Servings: 4

Ingredients:
- 12 large fresh oysters
- 12 slices of streaky bacon
- Lemon wedges, for garnish

Preparation Instructions:
1. Preheat the Ninja Air Fryer to 375°F using the

Bake mode.

2. Wrap each fresh oyster in a slice of streaky bacon and secure it with a toothpick.
3. Place the bacon-wrapped oysters in the air fryer basket.
4. Air fry the Angels on Horseback for about 5-7 minutes, or until the bacon is crispy and the oysters are cooked through.
5. Remove the Angels on Horseback from the air fryer and let them cool for a moment.
6. Serve the Angels on Horseback with lemon wedges for garnish.

Haggis Bon Bons

Prep Time: 20 minutes / Cook Time: 10 minutes / Servings: 4

Ingredients:
- 200g haggis
- 100g breadcrumbs
- 1 egg, beaten
- Cooking oil, for frying
- Optional: whisky sauce or a dipping sauce of your choice

Preparation Instructions:
1. Preheat the Ninja Air Fryer to 375°F using the Bake mode.
2. Take small portions of haggis and roll them into bite-sized balls.
3. Roll the haggis balls in beaten egg, ensuring they are well-coated.
4. Coat the haggis balls in breadcrumbs until they are fully covered.
5. Place the haggis bon bons in the air fryer basket.
6. Air fry the Haggis Bon Bons for about 7-10 minutes, or until they are golden brown and heated through.
7. Remove the Haggis Bon Bons from the air fryer and let them cool for a moment.
8. Serve the Haggis Bon Bons hot with a whisky sauce or a dipping sauce of your choice.

Blinis with Smoked Salmon

Prep Time: 20 minutes / Cook Time: 10 minutes / Servings: 4

Ingredients:
- For the Blinis:
- 100g all-purpose flour
- 1/2 teaspoon baking powder
- 1/2 teaspoon sugar
- 1/4 teaspoon salt
- 1 egg

- 150ml milk
- 1 tablespoon unsalted butter, melted
- Cooking oil, for greasing
- For the Topping:
- 150g smoked salmon
- Crème fraîche or sour cream
- Fresh dill, for garnish
- Lemon wedges, for serving

Preparation Instructions:
1. Preheat the Ninja Air Fryer to 375°F using the Bake mode.
2. In a mixing bowl, sift the all-purpose flour, baking powder, sugar, and salt.
3. In a separate bowl, whisk together the egg, milk, and melted unsalted butter.
4. Gradually pour the wet Ingredients into the dry Ingredients and whisk until you have a smooth batter.
5. Grease the air fryer basket or air fryer trays with a small amount of cooking oil.
6. Drop small spoonfuls of the blini batter onto the greased air fryer surface, leaving space between them.
7. Air fry the blinis at 375°F for about 5 minutes, or until they are puffed and golden.
8. Carefully remove the blinis from the air fryer and let them cool for a moment.
9. Top each blini with a piece of smoked salmon and a dollop of crème fraîche or sour cream.
10. Garnish with fresh dill and serve with lemon wedges on the side.

Bath Buns

Prep Time: 20 minutes / Cook Time: 20 minutes / Servings: 4

Ingredients:
- 500g all-purpose flour
- 1 packet (7g) active dry yeast
- 100g granulated sugar
- 1/2 teaspoon salt
- 200ml warm milk
- 100g unsalted butter, softened
- 2 eggs
- Currants or sultanas (for topping)
- Additional granulated sugar (for topping)

Preparation Instructions:
1. Preheat the Ninja Air Fryer to 375°F using the Bake mode.
2. In a small bowl, dissolve the active dry yeast in the warm milk. Let it sit for about 5 minutes until frothy.

3. In a mixing bowl, combine the all-purpose flour, granulated sugar, and salt.
4. Add the softened unsalted butter and eggs to the flour mixture. Mix well.
5. Pour the yeast mixture into the flour mixture and stir until you have a smooth dough.
6. Knead the dough on a floured surface for about 5-7 minutes until it's elastic and smooth.
7. Divide the dough into equal portions and shape them into buns.
8. Place the buns on a greased baking tray, leaving space between them.
9. Brush the buns with a little milk and sprinkle currants or sultanas and additional granulated sugar on top.
10. Bake the Bath Buns in the air fryer at 375°F for about 15-20 minutes or until they are golden brown and sound hollow when tapped on the bottom.
11. Remove the Bath Buns from the air fryer and let them cool for a few minutes.
12. Serve the Bath Buns warm or at room temperature.

Carrageen Moss Pudding

Prep Time: 10 minutes / Cook Time: 30 minutes / Servings: 4

Ingredients:
- 20g dried carrageen moss
- 500ml milk
- 30g granulated sugar
- 5g vanilla extract

Preparation Instructions:
1. Preheat the Ninja Air Fryer to 375°F using the Bake mode.
2. Rinse the dried carrageen moss under cold water.
3. In a saucepan, combine the carrageen moss and milk.
4. Bring the mixture to a boil and then simmer for about 20 minutes until the carrageen moss softens and swells.
5. Stir in the granulated sugar and vanilla extract.
6. Simmer for another 10 minutes until the pudding thickens.
7. Pour the Carrageen Moss Pudding into serving dishes.
8. Place the dishes in the air fryer.
9. Bake for about 10 minutes to heat the pudding through.
10. Remove from the air fryer and let it cool slightly before serving.

Jaffa Cakes

Prep Time: 20 minutes / Cook Time: 15 minutes / Servings: 4

Ingredients:
- 100g all-purpose flour
- 100g granulated sugar
- 3 large eggs
- 1/2 teaspoon baking powder
- 2 tablespoons orange marmalade
- 100g dark chocolate
- 2 tablespoons unsalted butter

Preparation Instructions:
1. Preheat the Ninja Air Fryer to 375°F using the Bake mode.
2. In a mixing bowl, beat the eggs and granulated sugar together until light and fluffy.
3. Sift in the all-purpose flour and baking powder, and gently fold them into the egg mixture.
4. Grease the air fryer tray or air fryer basket with a little oil.
5. Drop spoonfuls of the cake batter onto the tray or into the basket, leaving space between them.
6. Air fry the cakes at 375°F for about 10-15 minutes or until they are golden and springy to the touch.
7. Remove the cakes from the air fryer and let them cool for a moment.
8. Heat the orange marmalade in a microwave or on the stovetop until it becomes liquid.
9. Spoon a small amount of orange marmalade onto each cake and spread it evenly.
10. Melt the dark chocolate and unsalted butter together until smooth.
11. Pour the melted chocolate over the marmalade layer on each cake.
12. Allow the chocolate to set.
13. Serve the Jaffa Cakes as a delicious dessert.

Twiglets

Prep Time: 20 minutes / Cook Time: 15 minutes / Servings: 4

Ingredients:
- 200g whole wheat breadsticks
- 3 tablespoons Marmite (or similar yeast extract)
- 1 tablespoon olive oil

Preparation Instructions:
1. Preheat your oven to 350°F using the Bake mode.
2. In a microwave-safe bowl, combine the Marmite and olive oil. Microwave for a few seconds to

make it easier to mix.

3. Dip each whole wheat breadstick into the Marmite and olive oil mixture, ensuring they are evenly coated.
4. Place the coated breadsticks on a baking sheet lined with parchment paper.
5. Bake in the preheated oven for about 15 minutes or until the breadsticks become crispy.
6. Remove from the oven and let them cool.
7. Once cooled, your homemade Twiglets are ready to enjoy as a savory snack.

Nut Roast

Prep Time: 20 minutes / Cook Time: 45 minutes / Servings: 4

Ingredients
- 200g mixed nuts (such as almonds, cashews, and walnuts), roughly chopped
- 100g breadcrumbs
- 1 medium onion, finely chopped
- 1 clove garlic, minced
- 200g mushrooms, finely chopped
- 1 red bell pepper, finely chopped
- 2 tablespoons olive oil
- 2 tablespoons tomato paste
- 1 teaspoon dried thyme
- 1 teaspoon dried rosemary
- Salt and pepper to taste
- 2 eggs, beaten

Preparation Instructions:
1. Preheat the Ninja Air Fryer to 375°F using the Bake mode.
2. In a large skillet, heat the olive oil over medium heat. Add the chopped onion and garlic and sauté until they become translucent.
3. Add the chopped mushrooms and red bell pepper to the skillet. Cook for a few minutes until the mushrooms release their moisture and the mixture is softened.
4. In a mixing bowl, combine the chopped nuts, breadcrumbs, sautéed vegetable mixture, tomato paste, dried thyme, dried rosemary, salt, and pepper.
5. Mix in the beaten eggs, and combine all the Ingredients thoroughly to form a cohesive mixture.
6. Transfer the nut roast mixture into a greased baking dish or loaf tin.
7. Place the dish in the air fryer and bake for about 40-45 minutes until the nut roast is firm and the top is golden.
8. Remove the nut roast from the air fryer and let it cool for a few minutes.

9. Slice and serve the Nut Roast with your favorite vegetarian gravy and side dishes.

Cucumber Cream Cheese Tea Sandwiches

Prep Time: 15 minutes / Servings: 4

Ingredients:
- 8 slices of fresh white bread
- 4 ounces (about 115g) cream cheese, softened
- 1/2 cucumber, thinly sliced
- Fresh dill, for garnish (optional)
- Salt and black pepper to taste

Preparation Instructions:
1. Preheat the Ninja Air Fryer to 375°F using the Bake mode.
2. Spread a thin layer of softened cream cheese on one side of each slice of bread.
3. Arrange the thinly sliced cucumber on half of the bread slices, overlapping them to cover the entire surface.
4. Sprinkle a pinch of salt and black pepper on the cucumber slices.
5. Top the cucumber with the remaining slices of bread, cream cheese side down, to make sandwiches.
6. Cut off the crusts from the sandwiches for a classic tea sandwich look, if desired.
7. Cut each sandwich into halves or quarters to create smaller tea sandwiches.
8. Place the tea sandwiches in the air fryer basket.
9. Air fry the Cucumber Cream Cheese Tea Sandwiches at 375°F for about 3-5 minutes, or until they are heated through and the bread is slightly crispy.
10. Remove the tea sandwiches from the air fryer and let them cool for a moment.
11. Garnish with fresh dill if desired.

Fadge

Prep Time: 10 minutes / Cook Time: 15 minutes / Servings: 4

Ingredients:
- 500g potatoes, peeled and grated
- 50g all-purpose flour
- 1/2 teaspoon salt
- 1/4 teaspoon black pepper
- 2 tablespoons vegetable oil

Preparation Instructions:
1. Preheat the Ninja Air Fryer to 375°F using the Bake mode.

2. Place the grated potatoes in a clean kitchen towel or cheesecloth and squeeze out any excess moisture.
3. In a mixing bowl, combine the grated potatoes, all-purpose flour, salt, and black pepper. Mix well to form a dough.
4. Divide the dough into equal portions and shape them into flat cakes or patties.
5. Brush the air fryer basket or air fryer trays with vegetable oil to prevent sticking.
6. Place the potato cakes in the air fryer basket or on the trays, leaving space between them.
7. Air fry the Fadge at 375°F for about 12-15 minutes, or until they are golden brown and crispy.
8. Carefully remove the Fadge from the air fryer and let them cool for a moment.
9. Serve your Fadge as a delicious side dish or breakfast item.

Ginger Parkin

Prep Time: 15 minutes / Cook Time: 45 minutes / Servings: 4

Ingredients:
- 200g oatmeal
- 100g self-raising flour
- 2 teaspoons ground ginger
- 1 teaspoon ground cinnamon
- 100g butter
- 100g golden syrup
- 100g black treacle
- 100g brown sugar
- 1 egg, beaten
- 150ml milk

Preparation Instructions:
1. Preheat the Ninja Air Fryer to 375°F using the Bake mode.
2. In a mixing bowl, combine the oatmeal, self-raising flour, ground ginger, and ground cinnamon.
3. In a saucepan, melt the butter over low heat. Add the golden syrup, black treacle, and brown sugar. Stir until the mixture is well combined.
4. Remove the saucepan from heat and allow the mixture to cool slightly.
5. Pour the beaten egg and milk into the syrup mixture and whisk together.
6. Gradually add the wet Ingredients to the dry Ingredients and mix until you have a smooth batter.
7. Pour the batter into a greased and lined baking tin or dish.
8. Place the tin in the air fryer and bake for about 40-45 minutes, or until the parkin is firm and a skewer inserted into the centre comes out clean.
9. Remove the Ginger Parkin from the air fryer and

let it cool in the tin for a while before cutting into squares or slices.
10. Once cooled, serve your Ginger Parkin as a delightful treat.

Flapjacks

Prep Time: 15 minutes / Cook Time: 25 minutes / Servings: 4

Ingredients:
- 200g rolled oats
- 100g unsalted butter
- 75g granulated sugar
- 2 tablespoons golden syrup
- 1/2 teaspoon vanilla extract
- A pinch of salt

Preparation Instructions:
1. Preheat the Ninja Air Fryer to 350°F using the Bake mode.
2. In a saucepan, melt the unsalted butter, granulated sugar, golden syrup, vanilla extract, and a pinch of salt. Stir until well combined and smooth.
3. Add the rolled oats to the mixture and stir until the oats are evenly coated.
4. Grease the air fryer tray or basket with a little butter or oil.
5. Press the oat mixture into the tray or basket, creating a uniform layer.
6. Air fry the Flapjacks at 350°F for about 20-25 minutes or until they are golden brown.
7. Remove the Flapjacks from the air fryer and let them cool for a few minutes.
8. Cut the Flapjacks into squares or rectangles while they are still warm.
9. Allow the Flapjacks to cool completely before serving.

Bara Brith

Prep Time: 15 minutes / Cook Time: 55 minutes / Servings: 4

Ingredients:
- 250g mixed dried fruit
- 200ml strong tea
- 100g light brown sugar
- 1 large egg
- 300g self-raising flour
- 1/2 teaspoon mixed spice (cinnamon, nutmeg, allspice)
- Butter for greasing

Preparation Instructions:
1. Preheat the Ninja Air Fryer to 350°F using the Bake mode.

2. In a mixing bowl, combine the mixed dried fruit and strong tea. Let it soak for about 30 minutes.
3. Grease and line a loaf pan with butter.
4. In a separate bowl, beat the sugar and egg together until well combined.
5. Stir in the self-raising flour and mixed spice to form a batter.
6. Add the soaked fruit mixture to the batter and stir until everything is evenly mixed.
7. Pour the Bara Brith batter into the prepared loaf pan.
8. Place the loaf pan in the air fryer basket.
9. Air fry the Bara Brith at 350°F for about 50-55 minutes, or until it's cooked through and a toothpick comes out clean when inserted.
10. Remove the Bara Brith from the air fryer and let it cool in the pan for a few minutes.
11. Transfer the Bara Brith to a wire rack to cool completely.
12. Slice and serve your Bara Brith with butter, if desired.
13. Bara Brith is a traditional Welsh fruit bread that's perfect for tea time.

Dorset Apple Cake

Prep Time: 20 minutes / Cook Time: 45 minutes / Servings: 4

Ingredients:

- 200g all-purpose flour
- 1 1/2 teaspoons baking powder
- 1/2 teaspoon ground cinnamon
- 1/2 teaspoon ground nutmeg
- 1/2 teaspoon salt
- 100g unsalted butter, softened
- 150g granulated sugar
- 2 eggs
- 1 teaspoon vanilla extract
- 2 large apples, peeled, cored, and sliced
- 2 tablespoons milk
- 2 tablespoons demerara sugar (or brown sugar) for sprinkling

Preparation Instructions:

1. Preheat the Ninja Air Fryer to 375°F using the Bake mode.
2. In a mixing bowl, whisk together the all-purpose flour, baking powder, ground cinnamon, ground nutmeg, and salt.
3. In a separate bowl, cream the softened unsalted butter and granulated sugar until light and fluffy.
4. Beat in the eggs one at a time, ensuring they are fully incorporated. Stir in the vanilla extract.
5. Gradually add the dry Ingredients to the wet Ingredients and mix until you have a smooth cake batter.
6. Spread half of the cake batter in the bottom of a greased and lined cake tin.
7. Place a layer of sliced apples on top of the batter.
8. Add the remaining cake batter and arrange another layer of sliced apples.
9. Drizzle the milk over the top layer of apples, and sprinkle with demerara sugar.
10. Place the cake tin in the air fryer and bake for about 40-45 minutes, or until a skewer inserted into the centre comes out clean and the cake is golden brown.
11. Remove the Dorset Apple Cake from the air fryer and let it cool in the tin for a while before transferring it to a wire rack to cool completely
12. Serve and enjoy with family and friends.

Pikelets

Prep Time: 10 minutes / Cook Time: 10 minutes / Servings: 4

Ingredients:

- 200g self-raising flour
- 1 teaspoon baking powder
- 1 tablespoon granulated sugar
- 1 egg
- 250ml milk
- 1/2 teaspoon vanilla extract
- Butter or oil for greasing

Preparation Instructions:

1. Preheat the Ninja Air Fryer to 375°F using the Bake mode.
2. In a mixing bowl, sift the self-raising flour and baking powder. Stir in the granulated sugar.
3. In a separate bowl, beat the egg and then add the milk and vanilla extract. Mix well.
4. Gradually pour the wet Ingredients into the dry Ingredients and stir until you have a smooth batter.
5. Grease the air fryer basket or air fryer trays with a small amount of butter or oil.
6. Using a spoon, drop small rounds of batter onto the greased air fryer surface. Leave space between them to allow for spreading.
7. Air fry the pikelets at 375°F for about 5-7 minutes, or until they are golden brown and cooked through. You may need to cook them in batches depending on the size of your air fryer.
8. Carefully remove the pikelets from the air fryer and let them cool for a few minutes.
9. Serve your Pikelets with your choice of toppings, such as jam, butter, or syrup.

Tofu Roasted Croutons

Prep Time: 10 minutes / Cook Time: 20 minutes /
Servings: 4

Ingredients:

- 200g firm tofu, cut into small cubes
- 1 tablespoon olive oil
- 1/2 teaspoon garlic powder
- 1/2 teaspoon dried oregano
- 1/2 teaspoon dried thyme
- Salt and pepper to taste

Preparation Instructions:

1. Preheat the Ninja Air Fryer to 375°F using the Air Fry mode.
2. In a bowl, combine the tofu cubes, olive oil, garlic powder, dried oregano, dried thyme, salt, and pepper. Toss until the tofu is evenly coated with the seasonings.
3. Place the seasoned tofu cubes in the air fryer basket in a single layer.
4. Air fry for about 15-20 minutes, shaking the basket or tossing the tofu halfway through, until the tofu croutons are golden and crispy.
5. Once done, remove the tofu croutons from the air fryer and let them cool for a few minutes.
6. Serve the Tofu Roasted Croutons as a crunchy snack.

Forfar Bridies

Prep Time: 20 minutes / Cook Time: 30 minutes /
Servings: 4

Ingredients:

- 400g ground beef or minced beef
- 200g onions, finely chopped
- 200g potatoes, finely chopped
- Salt and pepper to taste
- 4 round pastry circles (shortcrust or puff pastry)
- Milk for brushing
- Optional: beef gravy or sauce for serving

Preparation Instructions:

1. Preheat the Ninja Air Fryer to 375°F using the Bake mode.
2. In a pan, cook the ground beef, chopped onions, and chopped potatoes until the meat is browned and the vegetables are tender. Season with salt and pepper.
3. Allow the meat and vegetable mixture to cool slightly.
4. Place a portion of the mixture on one half of each pastry circle.
5. Fold the pastry over the filling to create a semicircle shape. Seal the edges by crimping with a fork.
6. Brush the tops of the Forfar Bridies with a little milk to give them a golden finish.
7. Place the Forfar Bridies in the air fryer basket.
8. Air fry the Bridies at 375°F for about 25-30 minutes, or until they are golden brown and crispy.
9. Remove the Forfar Bridies from the air fryer and let them cool for a moment.
10. Serve the Forfar Bridies as a classic Scottish hand pie, with optional beef gravy or sauce on the side.

Okra Chips with Lemon Mayonnaise

Prep Time: 15 minutes / Cook time: 20 minutes /
Serves 5

Ingredients

- 1kg okra, cut into halves lengthwise
- 1 tbsp extra-virgin olive oil
- 1 tsp garlic granules
- 1 tsp onion powder
- 1 tsp ground coriander
- 1 tsp turmeric powder
- Sea salt and ground black pepper, to taste
- 100g breadcrumbs
- Lemon Mayonaisse:
- 2 egg yolks
- 1 tsp Dijon mustard
- 1 tbsp balsamic vinegar
- 1 salted anchovy
- 200ml olive oil
- 1 lemon, freshly squeezed
- 1 tsp dried dill weed
- Sea salt and red pepper, to taste

Preparation Instructions

1. Toss okra halves with olive oil, spices, and breadcrumbs until they are well coated on all sides.
2. Add okra to both drawers of your Ninja Foodi (with a crisper plate inserted).
3. Select zone 1 and pair it with "AIR FRY" at 180°C for 20 minutes. Select "MATCH" followed by the "START/STOP" button.
4. At the halfway point, shake the drawers to ensure even cooking; reinsert the drawers to resume cooking.
5. Meanwhile, make the lemon mayonnaise. Add egg yolks, mustard, vinegar, and anchovy to a bowl of your food processor; process until smooth paste forms.
6. Slowly and gradually, pour in the olive oil until the mixture becomes glossy and slightly thick. To finish, add lemon juice, dill, salt, and red pepper, and blitz for a few seconds more, until well combined.

7. Serve okra chips with lemon mayonnaise on the side and enjoy!

The Best Pigs-in-Blankets Ever

Prep Time: 10 minutes / Cook time: 15 minutes / Serves 6

Ingredients
- 12 cocktail sausages, casing removed
- 6 rashers pancetta, cut into halves lengthwise
- 1 tsp hot paprika

Preparation Instructions
1. Insert crisper plates in both drawers. Spray the crisper plates with nonstick cooking oil.
2. Wrap sausages in the pancetta slices and arrange them in both drawers if your Ninja Foodi.
3. Select zone 1 and pair it with "AIR FRY" at 180°C for 15 minutes. Select "MATCH" followed by the "START/STOP" button.
4. At the halfway point, turn the pigs-in-blankets over, and reinsert the drawers to resume cooking.
5. Sprinkle warm pigs-in-blankets with hot paprika and enjoy!

Banana Bread

Prep Time: 15 minutes / Cook time: 35 minutes / Serves: 4

Ingredients:
- 3 ripe bananas, mashed
- 80g unsalted butter, melted
- 100g granulated sugar
- 1 large egg
- 1 tsp vanilla extract
- 160g all-purpose flour
- 1/2 tsp baking soda
- 1/4 tsp salt
- 1/2 tsp ground cinnamon
- Chopped walnuts or chocolate chips (optional)

Preparation Instructions:
1. Preheat the Ninja Dual Zone Air Fryer to 160°C on zone 1 for 5 minutes.
2. In a bowl, mix together the mashed bananas, melted butter, granulated sugar, egg, and vanilla extract until well combined.
3. In a separate bowl, whisk together the flour, baking soda, salt, and ground cinnamon.
4. Gradually add the dry Ingredients to the banana mixture, stirring until just combined. Do not overmix.
5. Fold in the chopped walnuts or chocolate chips, if using.
6. Grease a loaf pan or silicone baking mould.

7. Pour the batter into the greased pan or mould, spreading it evenly.
8. Place the pan or mould in zone 1 of the air fryer and cook at 160°C for 35 minutes or until a toothpick inserted into the centre comes out clean.
9. Once cooked, remove the banana bread from the air fryer and let it cool in the pan or mould for a few minutes.
10. Transfer the banana bread to a wire rack to cool completely before slicing. Enjoy the moist and flavorful banana bread as a delightful snack or breakfast treat.

Pumpkin Spice Donut Holes

Prep Time: 15 minutes / Cook time: 10 minutes / Serves: 4

Ingredients:
- 150g all-purpose flour
- 80g granulated sugar
- 1 tsp baking powder
- 1/2 tsp ground cinnamon
- 1/4 tsp ground nutmeg
- 1/4 tsp ground cloves
- 1/4 tsp salt
- 60g pumpkin puree
- 60ml milk
- 1 large egg
- 1 tsp vanilla extract
- Icing sugar, for dusting

Preparation Instructions:
1. Preheat the Ninja Dual Zone Air Fryer to 180°C on zone 1 for 5 minutes.
2. In a bowl, whisk together the flour, granulated sugar, baking powder, ground cinnamon, ground nutmeg, ground cloves, and salt.
3. In another bowl, mix together the pumpkin puree, milk, egg, and vanilla extract until well combined.
4. Gradually add the wet Ingredients to the dry ingredients, stirring until just combined. Do not overmix.
5. Grease your hands with a little oil or butter.
6. Take small portions of the dough and roll them into small balls, creating donut holes.
7. Place the donut holes in zone 1 of the air fryer and cook at 180°C for 10 minutes or until golden brown and cooked through.
8. Once cooked, remove the pumpkin spice donut holes from the air fryer and let them cool for a minute.
9. Dust the donut holes with icing sugar before serving. Enjoy these bite-sized treats with the warm and comforting flavours of pumpkin spice.

Salted Caramel Popcorn

Ingredients:
- 60g popcorn kernels
- 50g unsalted butter
- 50g brown sugar
- 2 tbsp golden syrup
- 1/4 tsp sea salt

Preparation Instructions:
1. Preheat the Ninja Dual Zone Air Fryer to 200°C using the "FRY" function on zone 1.
2. Add the popcorn kernels to the crisper basket on zone 1 of the air fryer, making sure they are in a single layer.
3. Fry the popcorn kernels for 10 minutes, shaking the crisper basket occasionally, until all the kernels have popped.
4. While the popcorn is frying, make the salted caramel sauce by melting the butter in a small saucepan over low heat.
5. Add the brown sugar, golden syrup, and salt to the melted butter, and stir until combined.
6. Increase the heat to medium and bring the mixture to a boil, stirring constantly.
7. Remove the saucepan from the heat and pour the salted caramel sauce over the hot popcorn, stirring until all the popcorn is coated.
8. Spread the popcorn in a single layer on a baking sheet and allow it to cool for a few minutes before serving.

S'mores Empanadas with Marshmallow Filling

Ingredients:
- 1 sheet puff pastry, thawed
- 4 tbsp chocolate chips
- 4 tbsp mini marshmallows
- 1 small egg, beaten
- Graham cracker crumbs, for topping
- Powdered sugar, for dusting

Preparation Instructions:
1. Preheat the Ninja Dual Zone Air Fryer to 180°C on "BAKE" function.
2. Cut the puff pastry into 4 squares.
3. Place 1 tablespoon of chocolate chips and 1 tablespoon of mini marshmallows on each square.
4. Fold the puff pastry over the filling to create a triangle shape.
5. Use a fork to press down the edges and seal the empanadas.
6. Brush the empanadas with beaten egg and sprinkle graham cracker crumbs on top.
7. Place the empanadas in the air fryer and bake for 10 minutes or until golden brown.
8. Dust with powdered sugar before serving.

Chapter 8 Healthy Vegetarian and Vegan Recipes

Vegan Spinach & Feta Filo Parcels

Prep Time: 20 minutes / Cook Time: 15 minutes / Servings: 4

Ingredients:
- 200g fresh spinach, washed and chopped
- 100g vegan feta cheese, crumbled
- 1 small onion, finely chopped
- 1 clove garlic, minced
- 1 tablespoon olive oil
- 1 teaspoon dried oregano
- Salt and pepper to taste
- 4 sheets of vegan filo pastry
- 2 tablespoons melted vegan butter or olive oil (for brushing)

Preparation Instructions:
1. In a large pan, heat the olive oil over medium heat. Add the chopped onion and garlic and sauté until softened.
2. Add the chopped spinach to the pan and cook until it wilts and most of the moisture evaporates.
3. Remove the pan from heat, and transfer the cooked spinach and onion to a mixing bowl.
4. Add the crumbled vegan feta cheese, dried oregano, salt, and pepper to the bowl. Stir to combine the filling.
5. Preheat your Ninja Air Fryer to 375°F.
6. Lay out one sheet of filo pastry and brush it with melted vegan butter or olive oil.
7. Place another sheet of filo on top, offsetting it slightly to create a star shape.
8. Repeat with the remaining two sheets, so you have a layered star shape with eight points.
9. Place a portion of the spinach and feta filling in the centre of the filo star.
10. Gently fold the filo pastry over the filling, one section at a time, to create a parcel. Brush the top with more melted vegan butter or olive oil.
11. Place the parcels in the air fryer basket.
12. Air fry for about 12-15 minutes or until the filo pastry is golden and crispy.

Vegan Cornbread

Prep Time: 10 minutes / Cook Time: 20-25 minutes / Servings: 9

Ingredients:
- 120g cornmeal
- 120g all-purpose flour
- 50g granulated sugar
- 1 tablespoon baking powder
- 1/2 teaspoon salt
- 240ml almond milk or any other plant-based milk
- 60ml unsweetened applesauce
- 60ml vegetable oil (such as canola or corn oil)

Preparation Instructions:
1. Preheat your Air Fryer to 425°F and grease a baking dish.
2. In a large mixing bowl, combine the cornmeal, all-purpose flour, sugar, baking powder, and salt.
3. In a separate bowl, whisk together the almond milk, unsweetened applesauce, and vegetable oil.
4. Pour the wet Ingredients into the dry Ingredients and stir until just combined. Be careful not to overmix; a few lumps are okay.
5. Pour the cornbread batter into the greased baking dish.
6. Bake in the preheated Air Fryer for 20-25 minutes or until a toothpick inserted into the centre comes out clean and the top is golden brown.
7. Remove from the oven and let it cool for a few minutes before slicing and serving.

Pasta Primavera

Prep Time: 15 minutes / Cook Time: 20 minutes / Servings: 4

Ingredients:
- 300g pasta (of your choice)
- 60ml olive oil
- 2 cloves garlic, minced
- 150g cherry tomatoes, halved
- 100g asparagus, cut into 2-inch pieces
- 100g broccoli florets
- 100g red bell pepper, thinly sliced
- 75g carrots, thinly sliced
- 75g zucchini, thinly sliced
- 75g yellow squash, thinly sliced
- Salt and pepper to taste
- 30ml lemon juice
- 30g grated Parmesan cheese
- 10g fresh basil leaves, chopped

Preparation Instructions:
1. Preheat your Ninja Air Fryer to 375°F using the Air Fry mode.
2. Cook the pasta according to the package

instructions until al dente. Drain and set aside.

3. In a large bowl, toss the asparagus, broccoli, red bell pepper, carrots, zucchini, and yellow squash with 60ml of olive oil. Season with salt and pepper.
4. Place the seasoned vegetables in the air fryer basket.
5. Air fry for about 15-20 minutes, shaking the basket halfway through, until the vegetables are tender and slightly caramelised.
6. In a separate skillet, heat the remaining 30ml of olive oil over medium heat. Add the minced garlic and cook for about 1 minute until fragrant.
7. Add the cherry tomatoes to the skillet and cook for another 2-3 minutes, allowing them to soften.
8. Combine the cooked pasta, air-fried vegetables, and the tomato-garlic mixture in a large serving bowl. Toss everything together.
9. Drizzle lemon juice over the pasta and mix well.
10. Sprinkle the grated Parmesan cheese and chopped basil on top.
11. Serve your Pasta Primavera hot.

Roasted Butternut Squash and Chickpea Salad

Prep Time: 15 minutes / Cook Time: 25 minutes / Servings: 4

Ingredients:
- 400g small butternut squash, peeled and diced
- 425g can of chickpeas, drained and rinsed
- 30ml olive oil
- 5g cumin
- 5g paprika
- Salt and pepper to taste
- 200g mixed salad greens
- 30g feta cheese, crumbled
- 30ml balsamic vinegar

Preparation Instructions:
1. Preheat your Ninja Air Fryer to 375°F using the Air Fry mode.
2. In a large bowl, combine the diced butternut squash, chickpeas, olive oil, cumin, paprika, salt, and pepper. Toss to coat the squash and chickpeas evenly.
3. Place the seasoned butternut squash and chickpeas in the air fryer basket.
4. Air fry for about 20-25 minutes, tossing them halfway through, until the butternut squash is tender and slightly caramelised.
5. In the meantime, prepare the salad greens in a large bowl.
6. Once the roasted butternut squash and chickpeas

are done, let them cool slightly, then add them to the salad greens.
7. Drizzle the salad with balsamic vinegar and sprinkle with crumbled feta cheese.
8. Toss the salad gently to combine all the ingredients.
9. Serve the Roasted Butternut Squash and Chickpea Salad as a delicious and satisfying meal.

Spinach and Ricotta Cannelloni

Prep Time: 20 minutes / Cook Time: 30 minutes / Servings: 4

Ingredients:
- 12 cannelloni tubes
- 300g fresh spinach, chopped
- 250g ricotta cheese
- 30g grated Parmesan cheese
- 5g garlic powder
- 2. 5g nutmeg
- Salt and pepper to taste
- 475ml marinara sauce
- 60g shredded mozzarella cheese

Preparation Instructions:
1. Preheat your Ninja Air Fryer to 375°F using the Bake mode.
2. Cook the cannelloni tubes according to the package instructions until they are al dente.
3. In a mixing bowl, combine the chopped spinach, ricotta cheese, Parmesan cheese, garlic powder, nutmeg, salt, and pepper.
4. Carefully stuff the cooked cannelloni tubes with the spinach and ricotta mixture.
5. Spread a thin layer of marinara sauce on the bottom of a baking dish that fits in the air fryer.
6. Arrange the stuffed cannelloni in the baking dish.
7. Pour the remaining marinara sauce over the top.
8. Sprinkle the shredded mozzarella cheese over the sauce.
9. Place the baking dish in the air fryer and bake for about 20-25 minutes or until the cheese is bubbly and golden.
10. Remove from the air fryer and let it cool for a few minutes before serving.

Roasted Red Cabbage with Dijon

Prep Time: 10 minutes / Cook Time: 30 minutes / Servings: 4

Ingredients:
- 1 small red cabbage, thinly sliced
- 2 tablespoons olive oil
- 2 tablespoons Dijon mustard
- 1 tablespoon balsamic vinegar

- 1 teaspoon honey (or maple syrup for a vegan version)
- Salt and pepper to taste

Preparation Instructions:

1. Preheat your Ninja Air Fryer to 375°F using the Air Fry mode.
2. In a large bowl, combine the olive oil, Dijon mustard, balsamic vinegar, honey, salt, and pepper. Mix well to create a dressing.
3. Place the thinly sliced red cabbage in the bowl with the dressing and toss to coat the cabbage evenly.
4. Transfer the coated red cabbage to the air fryer basket.
5. Air fry the red cabbage for about 15-20 minutes, tossing it every 5 minutes for even roasting.
6. Check the cabbage for desired doneness. It should be tender and slightly crispy at the edges.
7. Once done, remove the roasted red cabbage from the air fryer.
8. Serve the Roasted Red Cabbage with Dijon as a flavorful main course side dish.

Caramelised Shallot and Feta Tart

Prep Time: 20 minutes / Cook Time: 25 minutes / Servings: 4

Ingredients:

- 1 sheet of puff pastry
- 6-8 shallots, peeled and sliced
- 1 tablespoon olive oil
- 1 teaspoon sugar
- 115g crumbled feta cheese
- 2 tablespoons fresh thyme leaves
- Salt and pepper to taste

Preparation Instructions:

1. Preheat your Ninja Air Fryer to 375°F using the Bake mode.
2. Roll out the puff pastry sheet and transfer it to a greased baking dish or tart pan. Prick the bottom of the pastry with a fork to prevent it from puffing up too much.
3. In a skillet, heat the olive oil over medium heat. Add the sliced shallots and sauté until they begin to caramelise, about 10 minutes. Sprinkle with sugar and continue to cook until they are nicely caramelised. Season with salt and pepper.
4. Spread the caramelised shallots evenly over the puff pastry.
5. Sprinkle the crumbled feta cheese and fresh thyme leaves over the shallots.
6. Place the tart in the air fryer basket and bake for about 15-20 minutes or until the pastry is golden

and the cheese is bubbling.
7. Remove the caramelised Shallot and Feta Tart from the air fryer and let it cool slightly before serving.
8. Cut into slices and enjoy.

Goulash

Prep Time: 15 minutes / Cook Time: 30 minutes / Servings: 4

Ingredients:

- 500g lean beef, cut into cubes
- 1 onion, chopped
- 2 cloves garlic, minced
- 2 red bell peppers, sliced
- 2 tablespoons sweet paprika
- 1 teaspoon caraway seeds
- 400g canned diced tomatoes
- 250ml beef broth
- 250g potatoes, peeled and diced
- Salt and pepper to taste
- 2 tablespoons olive oil
- Chopped fresh parsley for garnish

Preparation Instructions:

1. Preheat the Ninja Air Fryer to 375°F using the Air Fry mode.
2. In a large bowl, season the beef cubes with salt, pepper, and sweet paprika. Toss to coat evenly.
3. Heat 1 tablespoon of olive oil in a large skillet over medium heat. Add the beef and cook until browned on all sides. Remove and set aside.
4. In the same skillet, add the remaining 1 tablespoon of olive oil. Add the chopped onions and garlic. Sauté until the onions are translucent.
5. Stir in the sliced red bell peppers and caraway seeds. Sauté for a few more minutes.
6. Return the browned beef to the skillet and add the canned diced tomatoes and beef broth. Stir to combine.
7. Transfer the mixture to the air fryer basket. Add the diced potatoes.
8. Air fry for about 25-30 minutes, or until the beef is tender and the potatoes are cooked, stirring occasionally.
9. Garnish with chopped fresh parsley and serve your Goulash hot.

Vegan Cauliflower Alfredo

Prep Time: 10 minutes / Cook Time: 20 minutes / Servings: 4

Ingredients:

- 1 medium cauliflower (about 600g) chopped into florets

- 30ml olive oil
- 2 cloves garlic, minced
- 240ml unsweetened almond milk
- 15g nutritional yeast
- 15ml lemon juice
- 2. 5g salt
- 1. 25g black pepper
- 250g fettuccine or pasta of your choice
- Fresh parsley, for garnish (optional)

Preparation Instructions:

1. Preheat the Ninja Air Fryer to 375°F using the Air Fry mode.
2. Toss the cauliflower florets with 30ml (2 tablespoons) of olive oil and spread them evenly in the air fryer basket. Air fry for about 15-20 minutes, or until the cauliflower is tender and lightly browned.
3. While the cauliflower is roasting, cook the fettuccine or pasta according to the package instructions until al dente. Drain and set aside.
4. In a blender, combine the roasted cauliflower, minced garlic, 240ml unsweetened almond milk, 15g nutritional yeast, 15ml lemon juice, remaining 30ml of olive oil, 2. 5g salt, and 1. 25g black pepper. Blend until smooth and creamy.
5. Toss the cooked pasta with the cauliflower Alfredo sauce and heat them together in the air fryer for an additional 2-3 minutes until the sauce is heated through.
6. Garnish with fresh parsley, if desired.
7. Serve your delicious Vegan Cauliflower Alfredo meal hot.

Roasted Broccoli and Almonds

Prep Time: 10 minutes / Cook Time: 20 minutes / Servings: 4

Ingredients:

- 500g broccoli florets
- 60g whole almonds
- 2 tablespoons olive oil
- 2 cloves garlic, minced
- Salt and pepper to taste
- Zest from 1 lemon (optional)

Preparation Instructions:

1. Preheat the Ninja Air Fryer to 375°F using the Roast mode.
2. In a large bowl, toss the broccoli florets with olive oil, minced garlic, and whole almonds. Ensure they are evenly coated with the oil.
3. Season the mixture with salt and pepper to taste. You can also add lemon zest for extra flavor if

desired.
4. Place the seasoned broccoli and almond mixture in the air fryer basket in a single layer. You may need to do this in batches if your air fryer has limited space.
5. Roast the broccoli and almonds in the air fryer at 375°F for about 18-20 minutes, or until the broccoli is tender and slightly crispy, and the almonds are toasted. Be sure to shake the basket or toss the mixture once or twice during cooking for even browning.
6. Remove from the air fryer and serve.

Creamy Mushroom and Leek Puff Pastry Tart

Prep Time: 15 minutes / Cook Time: 25 minutes / Servings: 4

Ingredients:

- 1 sheet of puff pastry, thawed
- 200g mushrooms, sliced
- 2 leeks, trimmed and thinly sliced
- 2 cloves garlic, minced
- 2 tablespoons butter
- 2 tablespoons all-purpose flour
- 240ml vegetable broth
- 120ml heavy cream
- 1/2 teaspoon dried thyme
- Salt and pepper to taste
- 60g grated Parmesan cheese
- Fresh parsley, for garnish

Preparation Instructions:

1. Preheat the Ninja Air Fryer to 375°F using the Bake mode.
2. Roll out the puff pastry sheet on a lightly floured surface to fit a baking dish or tart pan. Place the pastry in the dish, trimming any excess and pressing it down to form the crust. Prick the bottom with a fork and set aside.
3. In a large skillet, melt the butter over medium heat. Add the sliced mushrooms and leeks, and sauté for about 5-7 minutes, or until they are softened.
4. Stir in the minced garlic and cook for another 1-2 minutes until fragrant.
5. Sprinkle the flour over the mushroom and leek mixture, and stir well to combine. Cook for a couple of minutes to eliminate the raw flour taste.
6. Gradually pour in the vegetable broth while stirring constantly. Then, add the heavy cream and dried thyme. Cook, stirring, until the sauce thickens, about 5-7 minutes. Season with salt and pepper to taste.

7. Pour the creamy mushroom and leek mixture over the puff pastry in the baking dish.
8. Sprinkle grated Parmesan cheese evenly over the top.
9. Place the baking dish in the air fryer basket and bake at 375°F for about 20-25 minutes, or until the puff pastry is golden and the tart is bubbling.
10. Garnish with fresh parsley before serving.
11. Slice and serve your delicious Creamy Mushroom and Leek Puff Pastry Tart.

Quinoa-Stuffed Bell Peppers

Prep Time: 20 minutes / Cook Time: 25 minutes / Servings: 4

Ingredients:
- 4 large bell peppers, any color
- 185g quinoa, rinsed and drained
- 475ml vegetable broth
- 1 can (15 oz or approximately 425g) black beans, drained and rinsed
- 165g corn kernels (fresh or frozen)
- 240g diced tomatoes (canned or fresh)
- 60g diced red onion
- 1 teaspoon ground cumin
- 1 teaspoon Chilli powder (adjust to your spice preference)
- Salt and black pepper to taste
- 120g shredded cheddar cheese
- Fresh cilantro leaves, for garnish

Preparation Instructions:
1. Preheat the Ninja Air Fryer to 375°F using the Air Fry mode.
2. Cut the tops off the bell peppers and remove the seeds and membranes. Set the bell peppers aside.
3. In a medium saucepan, combine the quinoa and vegetable broth. Bring to a boil, then reduce the heat, cover, and simmer for about 15 minutes, or until the quinoa is cooked and the liquid is absorbed. Fluff the quinoa with a fork and set it aside.
4. In a large mixing bowl, combine the cooked quinoa, black beans, corn kernels, diced tomatoes, diced red onion, ground cumin, Chilli powder, salt, and black pepper. Mix everything well to create the stuffing.
5. Stuff each bell pepper with the quinoa mixture, pressing it down gently.
6. Place the stuffed bell peppers in the air fryer basket.
7. Air fry the stuffed bell peppers for about 20-25 minutes, or until the peppers are tender and slightly charred.
8. Sprinkle shredded cheddar cheese over the tops of the bell peppers and air fry for an additional 2-3 minutes, or until the cheese is melted and bubbly.
9. Garnish the Quinoa-Stuffed Bell Peppers with fresh cilantro leaves before serving.
10. Serve these delicious stuffed bell peppers as a wholesome and satisfying meal.

Garlic and Herb Roasted Mushrooms

Prep Time: 10 minutes / Cook Time: 20 minutes / Servings: 4

Ingredients:
- 500g button mushrooms, cleaned and trimmed
- 2 cloves garlic, minced
- 2 tablespoons olive oil
- 1 tablespoon fresh thyme leaves
- 1 teaspoon dried oregano
- Salt and black pepper to taste
- Fresh parsley, for garnish

Preparation Instructions:
1. Preheat the Ninja Air Fryer to 375°F using the Air Fry mode.
2. In a large mixing bowl, combine the cleaned and trimmed button mushrooms with minced garlic, olive oil, fresh thyme leaves, and dried oregano. Toss everything to ensure the mushrooms are well coated with the seasonings.
3. Season the mushrooms with salt and black pepper to taste. Toss again to distribute the seasonings evenly.
4. Place the seasoned mushrooms in the air fryer basket in a single layer. You may need to do this in batches depending on the size of your air fryer.
5. Air fry the mushrooms for about 15-20 minutes, shaking the basket or turning the mushrooms halfway through to ensure even cooking. They should be tender and slightly browned.
6. Once done, remove the garlic and herb roasted mushrooms from the air fryer and transfer them to a serving dish.
7. Garnish with fresh parsley for a burst of color and flavor.
8. Serve the Garlic and Herb Roasted Mushrooms as a delightful meal.

Butternut Squash and Black Bean Enchiladas

Prep Time: 20 minutes / Cook Time: 25 minutes / Servings: 4

Ingredients:
- 1 small butternut squash (about 400g), peeled,

seeded, and cut into small cubes
- 1 can (15 oz or approximately 425g) black beans, drained and rinsed
- 1 red bell pepper, diced
- 1 small red onion, finely chopped
- 2 cloves garlic, minced
- 1 teaspoon ground cumin
- 1 teaspoon Chilli powder (adjust to your spice preference)
- Salt and black pepper to taste
- 240ml enchilada sauce
- 8 small corn tortillas
- 100g shredded cheese (such as cheddar or Mexican blend)
- Fresh cilantro leaves, for garnish
- Sour cream and sliced jalapeños (optional, for serving)

Preparation Instructions:

1. Preheat the Ninja Air Fryer to 375°F using the Air Fry mode.
2. In a large mixing bowl, combine the butternut squash cubes, black beans, diced red bell pepper, chopped red onion, minced garlic, ground cumin, Chilli powder, salt, and black pepper. Toss to coat everything with the spices and seasonings.
3. Place the seasoned butternut squash and black bean mixture in the air fryer basket. Air fry for about 15-20 minutes, or until the butternut squash is tender and slightly crispy.
4. While the filling is air frying, warm the corn tortillas according to the package instructions to make them more pliable.
5. Once the butternut squash and black bean mixture is done, remove it from the air fryer and let it cool slightly.
6. Pour a small amount of enchilada sauce into the bottom of a baking dish.
7. Take a tortilla, add a spoonful of the butternut squash and black bean mixture, roll it up, and place it seam side down in the baking dish. Repeat with the remaining tortillas.
8. Pour the remaining enchilada sauce over the rolled tortillas and sprinkle the shredded cheese on top.
9. Air fry the enchiladas for about 5-7 minutes, or until the cheese is melted and bubbly.
10. Garnish with fresh cilantro leaves and serve your Butternut Squash and Black Bean Enchiladas.

Okra and Tomato Curry

Prep Time: 10 minutes / Cook Time: 20 minutes / Servings: 4

Ingredients:

- 300g fresh okra, trimmed and cut into 1-inch pieces
- 2 large tomatoes, chopped
- 1 red onion, finely chopped
- 2 cloves garlic, minced
- 1 teaspoon ground cumin
- 1 teaspoon ground coriander
- 1/2 teaspoon ground turmeric
- 1/2 teaspoon Chilli powder (adjust to your spice preference)
- Salt and black pepper to taste
- 2 tablespoons vegetable oil
- Fresh cilantro leaves, for garnish

Preparation Instructions:

1. Preheat the Ninja Air Fryer to 375°F using the Air Fry mode.
2. In a mixing bowl, combine the fresh okra pieces with 1 tablespoon of vegetable oil and season with salt and black pepper.
3. Place the seasoned okra in the air fryer basket. Air fry for about 10-12 minutes, or until the okra is tender and slightly crispy. Make sure to shake the basket a couple of times during cooking.
4. While the okra is air frying, heat the remaining 1 tablespoon of vegetable oil in a skillet over medium heat. Add the chopped red onion and cook until it becomes translucent.
5. Stir in the minced garlic, ground cumin, ground coriander, ground turmeric, and Chilli powder. Cook for a few minutes until the spices are fragrant.
6. Add the chopped tomatoes to the skillet and cook until they soften and release their juices.
7. Once the okra in the air fryer is done, transfer it to the skillet with the tomato and spice mixture.
8. Mix everything well and let it simmer for about 5 minutes, allowing the flavors to meld.
9. Garnish with fresh cilantro leaves before serving your delicious Okra and Tomato Curry.

Eggplant and Halloumi Kebabs

Prep Time: 15 minutes / Cook Time: 15 minutes / Servings: 4

Ingredients:

- 1 large eggplant (aubergine), cut into 1-inch cubes
- 250g halloumi cheese, cut into 1-inch cubes
- 1 red bell pepper, cut into chunks
- 1 red onion, cut into chunks
- 2 tablespoons olive oil
- 1 teaspoon dried oregano
- 1 teaspoon paprika
- Salt and black pepper to taste

- Metal or wooden skewers (if using wooden skewers, soak them in water for 30 minutes before using)

Preparation Instructions:

1. Preheat the Ninja Air Fryer to 375°F using the Air Fry mode.
2. In a large mixing bowl, combine the eggplant cubes, halloumi cheese cubes, red bell pepper chunks, and red onion chunks.
3. Drizzle olive oil over the vegetable and cheese mixture. Add dried oregano, paprika, salt, and black pepper. Toss everything together to ensure even coating.
4. Thread the marinated eggplant, halloumi, bell pepper, and onion alternately onto metal or wooden skewers.
5. Place the skewers in the air fryer basket, leaving a bit of space between them.
6. Air fry the kebabs for about 12-15 minutes, turning them halfway through, until the vegetables are tender and the halloumi is slightly golden and crispy.
7. Remove the kebabs from the air fryer and let them cool for a minute before serving.
8. Enjoy your Eggplant and Halloumi Kebabs hot, with your favorite dipping sauce or alongside a fresh salad.

Sweet Potato and Quinoa-Stuffed Peppers

Prep Time: 15 minutes / Cook Time: 30 minutes / Servings: 4

Ingredients:
- 4 large bell peppers, any color
- 185g quinoa
- 480ml vegetable broth
- 2 medium sweet potatoes, diced
- 1 small red onion, finely chopped
- 2 cloves garlic, minced
- 1 teaspoon ground cumin
- 1 teaspoon paprika
- Salt and black pepper to taste
- 2 tablespoons olive oil
- Fresh parsley, for garnish

Preparation Instructions:
1. Preheat the Ninja Air Fryer to 375°F using the Air Fry mode.
2. Cut the tops off the bell peppers and remove the seeds and membranes. Set them aside.
3. In a saucepan, bring the vegetable broth to a boil. Add the quinoa, reduce the heat to low, cover,

and simmer for about 15-20 minutes, or until the quinoa is cooked and the liquid is absorbed.
4. In a mixing bowl, combine the diced sweet potatoes, chopped red onion, minced garlic, ground cumin, paprika, salt, black pepper, and olive oil. Toss to coat the sweet potatoes and seasonings.
5. Place the seasoned sweet potatoes in the air fryer basket and air fry for about 10-15 minutes until they are tender and slightly crispy.
6. In a large mixing bowl, combine the cooked quinoa and roasted sweet potatoes. Mix well.
7. Stuff each bell pepper with the quinoa and sweet potato mixture.
8. Place the stuffed peppers in the air fryer basket.
9. Air fry the stuffed peppers for about 10-15 minutes, or until the peppers are tender and slightly charred.
10. Garnish with fresh parsley and serve your Sweet Potato and Quinoa-Stuffed Peppers.

Roasted Pumpkin and Rocket Salad

Prep Time: 10 minutes / Cook Time: 25 minutes / Servings: 4

Ingredients:
- 500g pumpkin, peeled and cubed
- 2 tablespoons olive oil
- Salt and pepper to taste
- 240g rocket (arugula)
- 60g pumpkin seeds, toasted
- For the Dressing:
- 3 tablespoons extra-virgin olive oil
- 1 tablespoon balsamic vinegar
- 1 teaspoon honey
- 1 teaspoon Dijon mustard
- Salt and pepper to taste

Preparation Instructions:
1. Preheat the Ninja Air Fryer to 375°F using the Bake mode.
2. In a bowl, toss the cubed pumpkin with 2 tablespoons of olive oil and season with salt and pepper.
3. Place the pumpkin cubes in the air fryer basket.
4. Bake for about 20-25 minutes, or until the pumpkin is tender and slightly caramelised. Shake the basket occasionally for even cooking.
5. While the pumpkin is roasting, prepare the dressing. In a small bowl, whisk together 3 tablespoons of extra-virgin olive oil, 1 tablespoon of balsamic vinegar, 1 teaspoon of honey, 1 teaspoon of Dijon mustard, salt, and pepper. Set the dressing aside.
6. Once the pumpkin is done, remove it from the air fryer and let it cool slightly.
7. In a large bowl, combine the rocket (arugula) with

the roasted pumpkin cubes.

8. Drizzle the dressing over the salad and toss gently to coat the ingredients.
9. Sprinkle toasted pumpkin seeds on top for extra crunch.
10. Serve your Roasted Pumpkin and Rocket Salad as a delicious and healthy side or main dish.

Portobello Mushroom Steaks with Chimichurri

Prep Time: 10 minutes / Cook Time: 15 minutes / Servings: 4

Ingredients:

- For the Portobello Mushroom Steaks:
- 4 large Portobello mushrooms
- 30ml olive oil
- 2 cloves garlic, minced
- 5ml balsamic vinegar
- Salt and pepper to taste
- For the Chimichurri Sauce:
- 240 ml fresh parsley, finely chopped
- 60 ml fresh cilantro, finely chopped
- 2 cloves garlic, minced
- 60 ml red wine vinegar
- 120 ml extra-virgin olive oil
2. 5 ml red pepper flakes
- Salt and pepper to taste

Preparation Instructions:

1. Preheat the Ninja Air Fryer to 375°F using the Air Fry mode.
2. Clean the Portobello mushrooms and remove the stems.
3. In a small bowl, whisk together the olive oil, minced garlic, balsamic vinegar, salt, and pepper.
4. Brush the Portobello mushrooms with the olive oil mixture, ensuring they are well coated.
5. Place the mushrooms in the air fryer basket, cap side down.
6. Air fry for about 12-15 minutes, turning them halfway through, until the mushrooms are tender and slightly crispy.

7. While the mushrooms are air frying, prepare the chimichurri sauce. In a separate bowl, combine the chopped parsley, cilantro, minced garlic, red wine vinegar, extra-virgin olive oil, red pepper flakes, salt, and pepper. Mix well.
8. Once the Portobello mushroom steaks are done, remove them from the air fryer.
9. Serve the mushroom steaks with a generous drizzle of chimichurri sauce on top.
10. Enjoy your Portobello Mushroom Steaks with Chimichurri.

Parsnip and Apple Hash

Prep Time: 10 minutes / Cook Time: 20 minutes / Servings: 4

Ingredients:

- 4 parsnips, peeled and grated
- 2 apples, peeled, cored, and grated
- 1 small onion, finely chopped
- 2 tablespoons olive oil
- Salt and pepper to taste
- Fresh parsley, for garnish

Preparation Instructions:

1. Preheat the Ninja Air Fryer to 350°F using the Air Fry mode.
2. In a large bowl, combine the grated parsnips, grated apples, and finely chopped onion.
3. Season the mixture with salt and pepper.
4. Divide the mixture into four portions.
5. Brush the air fryer basket with olive oil to prevent sticking.
6. Place one portion of the parsnip and apple mixture in the air fryer basket.
7. Air fry for about 15-20 minutes, or until the hash is golden brown and crispy.
8. Repeat the process for the remaining portions.
9. Garnish with fresh parsley before serving your Parsnip and Apple Hash.

Chapter 9 Desserts

Shropshire Fidget Pie

Prep Time: 20 minutes / Cook Time: 40 minutes / Servings: 4

Ingredients:
- 400g pork shoulder, cubed
- 200g cooking apples, peeled and sliced
- 200g onions, chopped
- 200g potatoes, peeled and sliced
- 30g butter
- Salt and pepper to taste
- Prepared shortcrust pastry

Preparation Instructions:
1. Preheat the Ninja Air Fryer to 375°F using the Bake mode.
2. In a pan, melt the butter and sauté the onions until softened.
3. Add the cubed pork and brown it.
4. Layer the sliced potatoes, apples, and sautéed onions in a pie dish.
5. Place the browned pork on top and season with salt and pepper.
6. Cover the filling with the shortcrust pastry.
7. Bake until the pastry is golden brown and the filling is cooked through.

Blackpool Milk Roll

Prep Time: 15 minutes / Cook Time: 25 minutes / Servings: 4

Ingredients:
- 300g all-purpose flour
- 200ml whole milk
- 30g sugar
- 30g butter
- 7g active dry yeast
- 5g salt

Preparation Instructions:
1. In a mixing bowl, combine the flour, sugar, and salt.
2. Warm the milk and melt the butter. Add the yeast to the warm milk and let it sit for a few minutes until foamy.
3. Gradually add the milk mixture to the dry ingredients, kneading until you have a smooth dough.
4. Shape the dough into a roll and place it in a greased baking dish.
5. Preheat the Ninja Air Fryer to 375°F using the Bake mode.

6. Bake the milk roll for about 25 minutes or until it's golden brown and sounds hollow when tapped.
7. Allow it to cool before slicing.

Cumbrian Grasmere Gingerbread

Prep Time: 15 minutes / Cook Time: 20 minutes / Servings: 4

Ingredients:
- 200g self-raising flour
- 100g brown sugar
- 100g butter
- 2 tbsp golden syrup
- 1 tsp ground ginger
- 1/2 tsp baking soda

Preparation Instructions:
1. Preheat the Ninja Air Fryer to 350°F using the Bake mode.
2. In a saucepan, melt the butter and golden syrup over low heat.
3. In a mixing bowl, combine the self-raising flour, brown sugar, ground ginger, and baking soda.
4. Pour the melted butter and syrup mixture into the dry Ingredients and mix until you have a sticky dough.
5. Press the dough into a greased baking dish.
6. Air fry for about 15-20 minutes or until the gingerbread is golden and firm.
7. Allow it to cool before slicing into squares.

Liverpool Tart

Prep Time: 20 minutes / Cook Time: 30 minutes / Servings: 4

Ingredients:
- 200g shortcrust pastry
- 200g raspberry jam
- 200g fresh breadcrumbs
- 100g brown sugar
- 1 tsp mixed spice
- 100g butter, melted

Preparation Instructions:
1. Preheat the Ninja Air Fryer to 375°F using the Bake mode.
2. Roll out the shortcrust pastry and line a greased baking dish.
3. Spread the raspberry jam over the pastry.
4. In a bowl, combine the breadcrumbs, brown sugar, mixed spice, and melted butter.
5. Sprinkle this mixture over the jam.

6. Bake for about 30 minutes or until the tart is golden brown and set.
7. Allow it to cool before slicing.

Whim Wham

Prep Time: 15 minutes / Cook Time: 25 minutes / Servings: 4

Ingredients:
- 200g shortcrust pastry
- 200g raspberry jam
- 200g fresh breadcrumbs
- 100g brown sugar
- 1 tsp mixed spice
- 100g butter, melted

Preparation Instructions:
1. Preheat the Ninja Air Fryer to 375°F using the Bake mode.
2. Roll out the shortcrust pastry and line a greased baking dish.
3. Spread the raspberry jam over the pastry.
4. In a bowl, combine the breadcrumbs, brown sugar, mixed spice, and melted butter.
5. Sprinkle this mixture over the jam.
6. Bake for about 25 minutes or until the Whim Wham is golden brown and set.
7. Allow it to cool before slicing.

Bedfordshire Clanger

Prep Time: 20 minutes / Cook Time: 30 minutes / Servings: 4

Ingredients:
- 200g shortcrust pastry
- 200g minced beef
- 200g mashed potatoes
- 200g mashed sweet potatoes
- 100g onions, chopped
- 2 tsp lard
- Salt and pepper to taste

Preparation Instructions:
1. Preheat the Ninja Air Fryer to 375°F using the Bake mode.
2. Roll out the shortcrust pastry into a rectangle.
3. On one half of the pastry, spread the minced beef, mashed potatoes, and chopped onions. Season with salt and pepper.
4. Fold the other half of the pastry over the filling, creating a rectangular pie.
5. Seal the edges and make a few small slits on top.
6. Place the clanger in the air fryer basket.
7. Bake for about 30 minutes or until the pastry is golden brown and the filling is cooked through.

8. Allow it to cool before slicing.

Rhubarb and Custard Tart

Prep Time: 15 minutes / Cook Time: 30 minutes / Servings: 4

Ingredients:
- 200g shortcrust pastry
- 300g rhubarb, chopped
- 200g custard
- 100g sugar
- 2 eggs
- 1 tsp vanilla extract

Preparation Instructions:
1. Preheat the Ninja Air Fryer to 375°F using the Bake mode.
2. Roll out the shortcrust pastry and line a greased tart tin.
3. Spread the chopped rhubarb over the pastry.
4. In a bowl, whisk together the custard, sugar, eggs, and vanilla extract.
5. Pour this custard mixture over the rhubarb.
6. Bake for about 30 minutes or until the tart is set and the pastry is golden brown.
7. Allow it to cool before serving.

Manchester Tart

Prep Time: 20 minutes / Cook Time: 30 minutes / Servings: 4

Ingredients:
- 200g shortcrust pastry
- 200g raspberry jam
- 200g fresh breadcrumbs
- 100g brown sugar
- 1 tsp mixed spice
- 100g butter, melted

Preparation Instructions:
1. Preheat the Ninja Air Fryer to 375°F using the Bake mode.
2. Roll out the shortcrust pastry and line a greased tart tin.
3. Spread the raspberry jam over the pastry.
4. In a bowl, combine the breadcrumbs, brown sugar, mixed spice, and melted butter.
5. Sprinkle this mixture over the jam.
6. Bake for about 30 minutes or until the tart is golden brown and set.
7. Allow it to cool before slicing.

Cumberland Rum Nicky

Prep Time: 15 minutes / Cook Time: 25 minutes / Servings: 4

Ingredients:

- 200g shortcrust pastry
- 200g dates, chopped
- 100g mixed dried fruits
- 100g brown sugar
- 100g breadcrumbs
- 100g butter, melted
- 2 tbsp dark rum

Preparation Instructions:

1. Preheat the Ninja Air Fryer to 375°F using the Bake mode.
2. Roll out the shortcrust pastry and line a greased baking dish.
3. In a bowl, combine the chopped dates, mixed dried fruits, brown sugar, breadcrumbs, melted butter, and dark rum.
4. Spread this mixture over the pastry.
5. Bake for about 25 minutes or until the Rum Nicky is golden and set.
6. Allow it to cool before slicing.

Northumberland Singin' Hinnies

Prep Time: 15 minutes / Cook Time: 20 minutes / Servings: 4

Ingredients:

- 200g self-raising flour
- 100g butter
- 100g currants
- 100g sugar
- 1 egg
- 1/2 tsp nutmeg

Preparation Instructions:

1. Preheat the Ninja Air Fryer to 375°F using the Bake mode.
2. In a mixing bowl, rub the butter into the self-raising flour.
3. Stir in the currants, sugar, egg, and nutmeg to make a dough.
4. Roll out the dough and cut out rounds.
5. Place the rounds in the air fryer basket.
6. Air fry for about 20 minutes or until the Singin' Hinnies are golden and cooked through.
7. Serve warm with butter and jam.

Battenberg Cake

Prep Time: 30 minutes / Cook Time: 30 minutes / Servings: 4

Ingredients:

- 200g unsalted butter, softened
- 200g caster sugar
- 4 eggs

- 200g self-raising flour
- 1/2 tsp almond extract
- Pink and yellow food coloring
- Apricot jam
- 200g marzipan

Preparation Instructions:

1. Preheat the Ninja Air Fryer to 350°F using the Bake mode.
2. In a mixing bowl, beat the softened butter and caster sugar until light and fluffy.
3. Add the eggs one at a time, mixing well after each addition.
4. Stir in the self-raising flour and almond extract.
5. Divide the cake batter in half. Color one half pink and the other half yellow with food coloring.
6. Grease and line a square baking tin.
7. Spoon the pink mixture into one half of the tin and the yellow mixture into the other half.
8. Bake for about 30 minutes or until a skewer comes out clean.
9. Allow the cake to cool.
10. Trim the edges to make two even rectangles.
11. Warm the apricot jam and use it to sandwich the two cake pieces together.
12. Roll out the marzipan and wrap it around the cake to create a checkered pattern, then serve.

Banbury Cake

Prep Time: 20 minutes / Cook Time: 30 minutes / Servings: 4

Ingredients:

- 200g puff pastry
- 200g currants
- 100g raisins
- 100g mixed peel
- 100g brown sugar
- 100g butter
- 1 egg, beaten
- 1 tsp cinnamon
- Zest and juice of 1 lemon

Preparation Instructions:

1. Preheat the Ninja Air Fryer to 375°F using the Bake mode.
2. In a saucepan, melt the butter and add the currants, raisins, mixed peel, brown sugar, cinnamon, lemon zest, and juice.
3. Cook the mixture until the fruit is softened.
4. Roll out the puff pastry into a rectangle.
5. Spread the fruit mixture over the pastry.
6. Roll up the pastry to encase the filling and pinch the edges to seal.
7. Brush the top with the beaten egg.

8. Bake for about 30 minutes or until the Banbury Cake is golden brown and crisp.

Cornish Saffron Cake

Prep Time: 20 minutes / Cook Time: 25 minutes / Servings: 4

- 200g all-purpose flour
- 100g unsalted butter
- 100g sugar
- 2 eggs
- 1/2 tsp saffron threads, soaked in warm milk
- 1/2 tsp ground cinnamon
- 100g currants
- A pinch of salt

Preparation Instructions:

1. Preheat the Ninja Air Fryer to 375°F using the Bake mode.
2. In a mixing bowl, cream together the butter and sugar.
3. Add the eggs and mix until well combined.
4. Stir in the saffron milk and ground cinnamon.
5. Gradually add the flour and salt, mixing until you have a smooth dough.
6. Fold in the currants.
7. Shape the dough into a round and place it on a greased baking sheet.
8. Bake for about 25 minutes or until the Saffron Cake is golden and firm.
9. Allow it to cool before serving.

Melton Hunt Cake

Prep Time: 20 minutes / Cook Time: 30 minutes / Servings: 4

Ingredients:

- 200g self-raising flour
- 100g unsalted butter
- 100g sugar
- 2 eggs
- 1 tsp mixed spice
- 100g currants
- 100g raisins
- 100g sultanas
- 100g candied peel
- A little milk

Preparation Instructions:

1. Preheat the Ninja Air Fryer to 375°F using the Bake mode.
2. In a mixing bowl, cream together the butter and sugar.
3. Add the eggs and mix until well combined.
4. Stir in the mixed spice, currants, raisins, sultanas, and candied peel.
5. Gradually add the self-raising flour, mixing until you have a smooth dough. Add a little milk if the dough is too dry.
6. Shape the dough into a round and place it on a greased baking sheet.
7. Bake for about 30 minutes or until the Melton Hunt

Cake is golden and firm.
8. Allow it to cool before serving.

Yorkshire Parkin

Prep Time: 20 minutes / Cook Time: 30 minutes / Servings: 4

Ingredients:

- 200g oats
- 100g black treacle
- 100g golden syrup
- 100g butter
- 100g brown sugar
- 1 tsp ground ginger
- 1/2 tsp ground cinnamon
- 1/4 tsp ground nutmeg
- 1 egg

Preparation Instructions:

1. Preheat the Ninja Air Fryer to 350°F using the Bake mode.
2. In a saucepan, heat the black treacle, golden syrup, and butter until melted.
3. In a mixing bowl, combine the oats, brown sugar, ground ginger, ground cinnamon, and ground nutmeg.
4. Pour the melted mixture into the dry Ingredients and mix well.
5. Beat in the egg.
6. Grease and line a square baking tin.
7. Spread the Parkin mixture in the tin.
8. Bake for about 30 minutes or until the Yorkshire Parkin is firm.

Kentish Cherry Batter

Prep Time: 15 minutes / Cook Time: 25 minutes / Servings: 4

Ingredients:

- 200g self-raising flour
- 100g sugar
- 100g unsalted butter
- 2 eggs
- 100g cherries, pitted and halved

Preparation Instructions:

1. Preheat the Ninja Air Fryer to 375°F using the Bake mode.
2. In a mixing bowl, cream together the butter and sugar.
3. Add the eggs and mix until well combined.
4. Stir in the self-raising flour.
5. Gently fold in the cherries.
6. Grease and line a square baking tin.
7. Spread the Cherry Batter in the tin.
8. Bake for about 25 minutes or until the batter is golden and set.

Printed in Great Britain
by Amazon